ABOUT GRACE

ABOUT GRACE

BARBARA SHOUP

QUERENCIA

Querencia Press — Chicago IL

QUERENCIA PRESS

© Copyright 2024
Barbara Shoup

ISBN 978 1 963943 25 2

www.querenciapress.com

First Published in 2025

Querencia Press, LLC
Chicago IL

Printed & Bound in the United States of America

ALSO BY BARBARA SHOUP

Young Adult Fiction

Wish You Were Here
Stranded in Harmony
Vermeer's Daughter
Everything You Want
Looking for Jack Kerouac

Adult Fiction

Night Watch
Faithful Women
An American Tune

Nonfiction

Novel Ideas: Contemporary Authors Share the Creative Process
A Commotion in Your Heart: Notes on Writing and Life

For
Lyn Jones
&
Betsy Childers

CONTENTS

MORNING OF

It's two in the morning on what is without a doubt going to be the worst day of my life, and there's Kyle, tossing gravel at my bedroom window like we're in a bad movie. He's wearing a black hoodie, exactly like the one he gave me the night of our first break-in—and *shit,* suddenly I can feel his fingers pulling on the strings, covering everything but my nose and eyes, settling the hood on my head just right, then doing the same with his own.

"We're black holes," he said. "Invisible."

Which made me feel totally badass at the time, but now is clearly just one more example of why I have to make myself fall out of love with him.

I throw on the clothes I left in a puddle on the floor last night, tiptoe downstairs and out the door. It's late September, but still warm and muggy, bugs bouncing off the porch light. The street is empty, every window, dark. No sound but crickets singing. Kyle steps from behind the shrubbery, grinning that wicked, lopsided grin, and I have to stand there a long moment, arms folded on my chest, until rage wins against longing.

"Are you nuts?" I ask. "You need to get out of here. Now. If my mom wakes up, she'll call the police."

"Fuck that," he says. "I don't care what she does. I love you."

"Well, I don't love you back. Not anymore."

"Yeah, you do," Kyle says. "You know you do. Grace. Listen. I took all the money from my savings account. I've got a bag packed in my Jeep. Let's just get the hell out of here. You don't even need to go inside and get your stuff. Just come. We'll buy whatever you need."

"And go where?" I ask.

"I don't know yet. Somewhere."

Typical Kyle. He has no plan; he never had a plan. What does he imagine us doing when his money runs out? Robbing more houses?

Getting caught, *again?*

Still, every living bit of me wants to go with him—go, just go. Fuck everyone, everything. I'm scared to death to think about where I'm going to be this time tomorrow if I stay.

Kyle puts his arms around me, draws me close. "Amazing Grace," he whispers into my hair. "I love you so much. Come with me."

My head tucks perfectly into that familiar place just above his collarbone; my folded arms go slack, and I breathe in his Kyleness—coffee, sweat, soap and shampoo, a hint of weed. If I raised my face, he'd kiss me. I'd be lost.

"I have to go tomorrow," I say. "Can't you see I don't have a choice?"

"Bullshit," he says. "There's always a choice. So, choose us. We said forever, didn't we? Well, forever is now."

Forever is my needy, pathetic self. It's from this moment on, never, ever again taking risks because of what I felt—*feel*—about Kyle, because look where it got me.

I untangle myself from his arms and, not looking back, go inside, where I sit on my bed, heart hammering, tears streaming down my face, waiting—half-hoping for, half-fearing the sound of him banging on the door, calling my name.

But what I hear is Kyle gunning the engine of the Jeep, then screeching away.

ONE

Officer Snap

It's as cold as a meat locker in this closet-like room, where who knows how long ago a guard propped me on an orange plastic chair, my wrists burning under the cuffs, my legs still in shackles.

"Wait here," he said.

My wrist bones feel like they're breaking, but no way was I going to ask him to take uncuff me before he left. He wouldn't have done it anyway, and I'm not about to start off groveling no matter how bad they hurt or how freaked out they make me. I didn't ask for anything to drink, either, though my throat is so parched it hurts, and it's torture hearing the machine full of soda and water and iced tea humming just outside the door.

Breathe, I tell myself.

I breathe.

And remember the calming down trick Kyle taught me, something he learned from one, in the long line, of shrinks he'd seen since he was ten:

Focus on one small detail in your surroundings; breathe in/out, while looking at it. Then look at something else. Breathe in/out. Keep on.

Okay.

One single cement block in the wall. White, shiny. Little pock marks.

One high window framing a square of blue sky.

Smudged light switch with four screws.

My thumbnail with specks of purple nail polish on it.

The door opening.

A beefy White woman with spiky maroon hair.

Dark moons of sweat in her armpits.

A riot stick in a neat little holster on her belt.

She says nothing, just removes the handcuffs and shackles, then yanks me from the chair by my upper arm and walks me down a narrow corridor with rooms on either side. Girls peer from the small windows of their locked doors.

One voice. "Hey, Newbie. You scared?"

Another. "Don't worry, baby. I'll take care of you."

Laughter.

I keep my head down.

"Aw, come on, don't be unfriendly."

"Enough!" the guard bellows. "Next one who says a word gets written up. Move along, Lowery," she adds, nudging me forward with the flat of her hand.

We stop, finally, at a door marked "Intake. Mary Raab." The guard unclips a key ring from her belt, chooses a key, and opens it.

Another cold waiting room.

Another cement block wall: white, shiny, pock-marked.

Another orange plastic chair.

"Sit," the guard says.

I do. My fingers feel itchy for my phone and I move them, as if I'm typing on my thighs. Not like texting some ghost message, just to move my fingers in that familiar way. Through a barred window, I see a line of girls—twenty, thirty, I'm not sure; all wearing baggy khakis and green polo shirts or sweatshirts, all looking straight forward, their hands clasped behind them, disappearing one by one into a long, low building.

I hear a faraway voice. Indistinguishable.

Then the guard claps her hands right in front of my face.

"I am talking to you, Lowery," she says. "When I talk, you listen. Understand?"

I shudder, breathe back the rush of adrenalin telling me to jump up and go nose-to-nose with her. *Fucking bitch.*

Letitia Snap, that's the guard's name. It's on her badge.

"I *asked*, 'Do you understand me?'"

Letitia Snap? Kyle's voice. *Is that hilarious, or what?*

And, shit, I'm smiling.

Officer Snap stares at me, one hand on her stick, still in its holster. "You're amused to be here?"

I just stare back at her.

What nobody knows—not my parents or my vile stepmother, or the shrinks or the lawyer or the fucking judge or dogface Officer Snap—is that nobody can hurt me, not really, not anymore.

Intake

Ms. Raab, a plain, pasty woman, opens the door to the intake office. No smile, no welcome. Just one question after another and the clicking of her keyboard as she takes down my responses. Fine by me. I have no desire whatsoever to chat with anyone.

"Can you tell me your name, the date, and where you are?"

"Grace Lowery. October 14th. Prison."

"Madison Valley Juvenile Correctional Facility."

"Right," I say. "*Prison.*"

Ms. Raab pauses—her jaw tensing for just an instant—then types what I figure is the first black mark against me.

"Have you ever been in treatment for depression?"

"No."

"Have you taken any medications for depression in the past?"

"No."

"Are you taking any medications for depression now?"

"No."

"Have you ever been the victim of physical or sexual abuse?"

"No."

"Have you experienced any major losses or deaths in the last year?"

"No."

"Have you used alcohol and/or drugs in the last month?"

"Yes."

"Have you ever harmed yourself or engaged in risky behavior?"

"Well, *yeah*," I say. "I stole. I mean, that's how I got here."

Ms. Raab pauses again. "Just answer the question, please."

"Okay, sure. Yes. I have."

"And have you harmed yourself physically?

"Yes."

"Do you have a plan for harming yourself now?

I shrug.

"*Answer*, please."

"No."

"Have you ever tried to kill yourself?"

Like she doesn't know. Every single thing about me is in the thick folder on her desk, stuff I'm not even allowed to know myself. Therapists, police, juvey officers, inkblot tests, and personality indexes. Cutting. One pathetic suicide attempt.

"Grace?"

"Yes, I have tried to kill myself."

"Have you thought about killing yourself recently?"

"No. I haven't."

For a few moments, there's nothing but the sound of Ms. Raab typing, who knows what. Then she says, "Look at the red light on my computer. Don't smile."

No problem there, I think. The light flashes and, in moments, a blue security bracelet emerges—plastic, like the ones you get at concerts. I've got a bunch of them pinned to my bulletin board from shows I went to with Kyle. One, a VIP bracelet from when his dad got us backstage passes for Billie Eilish, I left on for days.

Ms. Raab comes from behind her desk and secures the bracelet to my right wrist. "You'll wear this at all times," she says. "When you transition from intake, you'll be issued a new one—red, high risk; yellow, medium; green, low—depending on an assessment of your behavior during that time. Do you have any questions?"

"No questions," I say. Jesus. Where would I even start?

"All right, then. We need to do a strip search."

I take a deep breath and blow it out. *You knew this was coming*, I tell myself. *Endurance, right? It's all about that.* Shit. "Endure" is the tattoo I *should* have gotten—on the inside of my wrist where I could see it when I needed it. Like now. I'm practically shaking with rage. *Worse* than rage, whatever worse than rage might be. Right now, Kyle is on his way to his stupid, fucking hippie school for troubled boys in Colorado. Or maybe he just kept driving last night. Fuck him, either way.

"I won't touch you and it will be private, just the two of us," Ms. Raab says, softening slightly, closing and locking the bathroom door behind us.

It's all stainless steel in here—the sink and countertop, the open shower stall. Even the mirrors, where I see a blurred reflection of myself: pale, sullen, my curly black hair wild and unkempt.

"Begin with your hoodie, please," Ms. Raab says, all business again.

I take off my zip-up hoodie, my vintage Black Sabbath tank top under it, my jeans, handing them to Ms. Raab, who folds them and puts them in a pile, logging each item onto a form on her clipboard. I kick off my flip-flops. Unhook the lacy black bra Kyle bought me, dangle it from my fingertips. I step out of the matching black thong.

Then stand, shivering, while she notes the marks on my body on her clipboard:

The one on my right eyebrow from when my mom slapped me so hard I fell against the bathroom faucet

The thin, white, vertical scar on my right forearm.

A pattern of scars, like pick-up sticks, on the inside of my thighs.

21

The Chinese character tattooed at the base of my spine.

Everything gets recorded, except for the bruise Officer Snap made on my upper right arm.

I watch her remove the last of the purple polish from my fingers.

Turn, bend from the waist, separate my butt cheeks when she tells me to—and feel her looking.

"All right, you can stand now," she says—adding, not unkindly, "We're almost finished." She hands me the clipboard. "Sign this if you agree that the list of marks on your body is correct, then hold the clipboard to your chest."

I sign, hold up the clipboard with my arms close to my body, covering my breasts the best I can, and Ms. Raab snaps a picture of the list with her iPhone.

Bunk Fifteen

I leave intake dressed in the orange polo shirt and sweats that all newbies wear until they transition from intake, worn-out work boots pinching my toes. I'm carrying the pile of hand-me-down clothes I was issued: a second set of orange sweats, a second orange polo shirt, two ratty white tee-shirts, a pair of scruffy sneakers, a pair of Brand X shower sandals, socks, underwear. Coat, gloves, hat, thermals for the cold weather coming. Officer Snap keeps a firm grip on my upper arm, deepening the bruise there, as we walk toward the cluster of low dormitory buildings.

Cottages, she calls them—

Probably where the crazy people lived when this place was the Wabash Valley Hospital for the Insane, I think. Kyle Googled the prison when he found out I'd be coming here, but I wouldn't let him tell me any more than that. I didn't want to know. But now that I'm here, I can't help wondering if the compound was surrounded by the same kind of high fence with rolls of spiky concertina wire along the top that surrounds it now. If the patchy grass was ever lush and green, the white trim on the red brick cottages was ever bright, unpeeling.

There's a patch of woods just beyond the part of the fence I can see. I hear dogs barking but can't tell where the noise is coming from. Do people live nearby? What would it be like for kids to grow up so close to a prison, I wonder—even if it's only a prison for a bunch of girls?

Correctional Facility. That's the official term for what this place is: Wabash Valley Correctional Facility for Girls.

Kyle laughed when he heard it. "What?" he said. "They're going to *correct* you? Like you're math homework?"

It pissed me off at the time. Easy for him to joke about where I was going, right? But, okay, it's pretty funny. Kyle's funny. Another thing I need to forget about him.

Officer Snap presses a button at the entrance of Cottage Five. "Snap. Delivery."

Like I'm a package.

A buzzing sound, a click. A Black woman opens the door.

"Grace Lowery." Officer Snap hands her my folder.

The woman, Officer Hadley, takes it and nods at me to step inside. She touches my bruised arm, but gently. "Cottage Five will be your home while you're here," she says. "There are rules, of course, but if you follow them, if you cooperate with the staff, you'll see that we do our best to make your time here go as well as it can. I'll show you your room and get you settled."

A dozen or so girls in a big room beyond the guard station watch as I follow her down a corridor lined with doors on either side. More white cement block walls. Black-and-gray speckled floor, grimy at the edges.

Officer Hadley stops to show me where the communal bathroom is—stainless steel, like Ms. Raab's bathroom, no curtains on the row of shower stalls. Then she stops again and unlocks the door to a room smaller than my stepmother's walk-in closet. There's an unmade bed, sheets, a green army blanket, a towel and washcloth folded at the foot. Six hooks on the wall, a shelf with two plastic bins for my belongings. No window. The red eye of a surveillance camera blinks above the door.

I put my crappy clothes into one of the bins. Officer Hadley waits while I make up the bed. No pillow, just a curved bump at the top end that makes my neck hurt just to look at it.

No roommate, though. One good thing.

"They'll bring your personals over later," Officer Hadley says.

"I don't have any."

"Well, you'll collect some over time, I expect, and the shelf over the desk, that's where they'll go. All right then, I'll take you back to the day room to meet the girls before dinner. You're bunk fifteen, by the way. We always line up and move in bunk order. You all right?" Officer Hadley adds.

I nod, though I'm filled with dread. Ever since my sentencing, I've been dreaming about locked-up girls, faceless, menacing. The worst thing is, my sister Briony is with me in the dreams—defiant—and I have to grab her, twist her arm until she cries to keep her from lunging at them. I had the dream last night too, after Kyle left, and woke up, like always, scared to death. When I finally calmed down, I got out of bed and put away the selfie of the two of us that Briony took the last time we were together. It was the only thing I planned to bring with me but it suddenly seemed like just taking a picture of her to such a place could hurt her somehow.

I take in the dayroom as Officer Hadley introduces me. Worn plaid couches, a couple of ratty armchairs, and a stack of plastic chairs. A blaring television. A low bookshelf with tattered paperback books and board games in beat-up boxes. A barred window framing the high fence and trees beyond.

Around a dozen girls quit what they're doing and stare at me, some, with a hint of threat. Officer Hadley says their names, which I immediately forget. Except Wren. Such a strange name. And she's tiny, so pale she's almost blue, with long, perfectly straight, white-blond hair that falls like a curtain around her face. She'd make a good Luna Lovegood, I think, then see the book she's hunched over is *Harry Potter and the Order of the Phoenix.*.

"Wren?" Officer Hadley repeats.

She looks up, preternaturally alert. Her pale turquoise eyes are so large they take up most of her face..

Officer Hadley gestures toward the empty place on the sofa beside her. "Be good for you to sit here awhile with the others before dinner's called," she says. "You've had a long day."

I sit. "I read that book," I say to Wren. "Like ten times. What do you think about J.K. Rowling? I mean, what she says about Trans people?"

She ignores me.

"Where you from?" one of the Black girls asks.

"Indianapolis."

"Huh. Not *my* neighborhood."

A pudgy White girl calls out, "You got kids?"

"Kids?" I ask.

A girl snorts. "Yeah, kids. You know. Short people who cry all the time?"

"Nope. No kids," I say.

"Smart." She nods at the pudgy girl. "Unlike Jessica here."

"I've got a beautiful little boy," Jessica says. "Damien—who hardly ever cries—and I wouldn't trade him for anything. He's almost two. Big for his age." She smiles, revealing brown, broken-off meth teeth. "Seriously, he's as big as his three-year-old cousin! And *strong*. You should see him. He's so cute, my cousin Bryce taught him to show his muscles." Her voice wavers, "It just kills me to be away from him, you know?"

"*Girl?* We trying to watch a show here," the Black girl—maybe Lauvette—says, saving me from a response.

She's sitting with two other Black girls on a couch directly in front of the blaring television, arms folded across their chests. Two skinny White girls sit on plastic chairs, scootched as close together as they can be. A couple of others are bent over doing homework at tables dotting the room. One's a cutter, her arms striped with wounds, scabs, and scars. Rail thin. A knife dripping with blood poorly tattooed just above her ankle.

I think of Kyle pulling up his sleeve to show me the tattoo of the Chinese character for chaos on his bicep not long after we got together. "Nietzsche," he said. "'I say unto you: one must still have chaos in one to give birth to a dancing star.'"

I was such an idiot. I should have known *right* then not to get mixed up with him—not to mention let him talk me into getting the same tattoo at the base of my spine.

Still, the character is so elegant. So cool, the way it actually looks like chaos, all black hooks and thorns about to fly off in every direction.

Gray Meatloaf

When we line up for dinner, Jessica calls out, "Fourteen," and steps in front of me, the look on her face so open and hopeful I can hardly keep from groaning.

Officer Hadley unlocks the door and we count off as we pass through. Then we count ourselves again, into the dining hall. We line up to receive our plastic trays of food, then carry them to long tables where we sit, eyes forward, forced to look at the collection of idiotic posters on the walls.

Discipline is the guardrail on the path to self-esteem.

A leader is one who knows the way, goes the way, and shows the way.

Don't make excuses, make improvements.

Be a buddy, not a bully.

Everyone smiles in the same language.

A lot like the posters I saw in my counselor's office every time she called me in last spring to ask why my grades were plummeting.

"Help me help you, Grace," she'd say. "You've always been such a good student. Tell me what happened to make this change."

I'd sit there until she sighed and let me go.

Dinner is gray meatloaf and fake mashed potatoes smothered in nasty gravy, mushy carrots, watery chocolate pudding for dessert. The lingering smell of a hundred other awful meals all mixed together. Jessica gazes at me longingly when I put my spork down, meal half-eaten.

But no sharing. Which, okay, is a nice irony, since aren't we supposed to learn to be more, not less, civilized here?

Back in the day room, Officer Hadley hands out little paper cups one at a time, watching each girl tip the pills in them to her mouth and swallow. "Meds," she says, setting one down at my place with just one pill inside.

I don't take any meds. But when I tell her, she says, "Everyone takes meds for sleeping here. Sometime during orientation you'll meet with the psychologist, who'll decide what else you need to take—and you'll take those pills, too.

I'm about to protest when I realize all the other girls are looking at me, waiting to see what I'll do—I pop the blue pill into my mouth.

It kicks in fast, or maybe I'm just tired for real. It's been a long, crappy day. I try staring at the TV, a rerun of "Friends," but I keep nodding and jerking back up—that half-sick from exhaustion feeling, and I'm not the only one. I watch the other girls dulling, their personalities going flat. Amber picks absentmindedly at her scabs. Wren closes her book, lays it on her lap. Jessica's chatter slows, her eyes glaze over. One by one, the homework girls put their heads down on the table.

Lights Out

Jack's big, rough hands nearly cover my small chest, fingers rubbing, pressing, pinching my girl places, and I stay as still as I can beneath him.

"If you tell anyone, I will kill you."

I feel the words enter my throat and coil up at the base of it: black, old-fashioned cursive letters lengthening, swelling, unwrapping themselves into a long rope that winds around and around my neck.

I bolt awake, screaming.

A key turns; a door opens. A voice speaking my name.
I shrink into myself, heart pounding, hands covering my face.
But it's not Jack's voice; it's a woman's, vaguely familiar, saying, "You're dreaming. Wake up now. Grace. You're dreaming."
Officer Hadley.
"It's okay," she says, kneeling beside me. "You're safe. Do you know where you are?"
I nod.
"Are you all right?"
I nod again, though I'm not all right at all.
"Good," Officer Hadley says. "You're safe here. I promise you. Try to go back to sleep."

TWO

Electra

There are just two of us waiting in the small orientation classroom: me and a girl with orange hair—real, it must be, because Jessica told me that anyone who comes in with weird hair gets a buzz-cut. Plus, the girl is covered in freckles.

"Electra," she says. "You?"

"Grace."

"So, what did *you* do to end up in this shit hole?" she asks.

That question is off-limits. One thing I've figured out is that there are unofficial rules about what you can and cannot say, a big one being do not ask about a person's crime. So, I ignore her. We're not supposed to be talking, anyway. Actually, as far as I can tell, we're not supposed to talk at all here. Fine with me.

"You don't have to take their shit," Kyle said when I was sentenced. "Remember who you are: Amazing Grace. You don't have to take shit from anyone."

But after three days locked up, any idea of rebellion I might have had has shriveled into a knot of anxiety in the pit of my stomach. And the last thing I need is to get sucked in by the energy swirling around this girl like tiny, gleaming knives.

Finally, a tall thin woman with a silver crew-cut appears and sits at the head of our table. "I'm Officer Martin. I'll be facilitating your movement through orientation." Then she hands each of us a copy of the *Wabash Valley Juvenile Correctional Facility Student Handbook,* and proceeds to read it aloud.

Personal Behavior

Behavior in Common Areas

Behavior during Movement Throughout the Facility

Personal Boundaries

Security and Control

Commissary

Contraband

Personal Hygiene

An interminable, utterly predictable droning, punctuated by, "Questions? Questions?"

Neither one of us speaks.

It's hot in the room. I'm drowsy. My eyes keep closing. Electra's, too, but she makes the mistake of putting her head down on the table, like you'd do at regular school.

Officer Martin stops in the middle of a sentence, stands, reaches over, and yanks her head up by the hair.

"Ouch," Electra says. "Fuck!"

"You will pay attention at all times," Officer Martin says. "All. Times. And did I not just go over rules for individual behavior? 'No inappropriate or foul language.' Is there something you don't understand about that?"

Electra rolls her eyes, lets out a stagy sigh.

Officer Martin narrows her eyes. "That is one demerit. Already. It's your choice, ladies," she says—like I'm in trouble, too. "You're not at summer camp. Do you understand that?"

"Yeah," Electra mutters.

"Yes," says Officer Martin. "Ma'am. Yes, Ma'am."

"Yes. Ma'am."

"Grace."

"Yes, Ma'am," I say.

Wide awake now, as scared as I was by last night's dream about Jack, I sit up straight to receive the rest of the Litany of Don'ts.

Jack Camp

Jack was my Aunt Marjorie's boyfriend. He lived in a blue house, the color of the violets that came up in the spring. When the big tree in his front yard made tiny green bouquets before the leaves came. It was a maple tree, he told me. After the leaves came, little pods with wings spiraled down like helicopters and covered the sidewalk and got in my hair and on my clothes when I was playing under it. Inside each one was the promise of a maple tree, Jack said. It's how maple trees got to be all over the neighborhood: the spinners flew off in the wind and fell down and dirt covered them, and maple trees grew.

He was a science teacher so he knew everything about nature. There was a special room in the blue house with bookshelves all the way up to the ceiling for his science books and his collections of rocks, shells, and geodes. One flat stone had the skeleton of a fish pressed into it, which Jack said was a fossil and was millions and millions of years old.

He said, "That fish was alive when dinosaurs were alive!"

He let me hold it, but always said, "Be careful!"

And I always was.

There was an aquarium full of brightly colored fish, and a microscope, which he let me put ordinary things under, like a strand of my hair or a sequin or a goldfish cracker. I'd look at them, thrilled by their strangeness.

The room had a big, cozy chair in it and a desk that was always piled with books and papers. Jack put a little desk in there for me too, and I worked when he worked, propping my stuffed animals against the wall and teaching them what Jack had taught me, then collecting their papers and scribbling grades on them at my desk.

I started going to his house every summer morning after my Nana died. I couldn't stay home because my mom worked and also went to college. I couldn't go to my dad's because he worked too, and he had a new wife, Marlys, who needed quiet.

Jack said, "Never mind. We'll have Jack Camp. Just you and me."

"He is a godsend," my mom said—even though she didn't believe in God anymore, which I knew because I heard her say it to Aunt Marjorie.

In the mornings, we worked in Jack's garden. Jack taught me which plants were weeds and which were vegetables. I went along each row pulling the weeds up and putting them in a red bucket, which he emptied into a big plastic bag when it was full. He took me to the flower store and let me pick out seeds I liked for a little garden of my own. He got me a straw hat for keeping the sun out of my face and a pair of purple gloves to wear for digging and planting so my hands wouldn't get dirty.

We went on nature hikes and to museums and bowling. We went to the swimming pool every single day it didn't rain. Before we went into the water, Jack rubbed sunscreen all over my body to be sure I wouldn't get a sunburn. After we jumped in, he put his hands on my arms and made swirling circles in the water with me. Sometimes threw me up and caught me, which always made me laugh and scream. But I loved it most when he floated me, holding me by my shoulders and my bottom and I closed my eyes and made my whole body go limp while the cool water lapped over me and I pretended I was floating down a river.

It was resting time in Jack's special bedroom when we got back from the pool. He read me a story, then lay down next to me and rubbed my back until I fell asleep. It was dark in the room, even in the daytime, but Jack put an Elmo nightlight in it so I wouldn't be afraid.

I loved Jack Camp so much that I cried when it was time to go back to school, even though I was very excited about going to the first grade and learning to read. When Jack found out I was sad, he hugged me and said, "No problem. We'll have Jack Camp *after* school. How about that?" And kept hugging me, combing my long hair with his fingers, and giving me little kisses on the top of my head and I felt happy and melty inside.

I drew him a picture: a big blue swimming pool with him in it, floating me, and a big yellow sun and both of us smiling.

What You Need to Know About Families

It's Leisure Time, and Jessica plops down beside me, already talking.

"Don't look, but that girl over there, Maria? The one at the table? She's been watching you. And those other girls with her? Bree and Amber? Maria's got a family with them. She's, like, the mom and they're her kids. They have to do what she says. And she's been watching you, like she wants you, too. What?" she adds, when she sees I'm smiling.

"It's not a problem," I say. "I told her I have AIDS."

Advice from Electra.

"That's not funny," Jessica says.

"It worked, though. It scared the shit out of her."

"You have to be careful here, Grace."

33

"Right," I say. "I know."

"Like, for example, you might think Wren is just a weird girl who reads all the time, but she's a murderer."

"Wren?"

"Yes, Wren. She *literally* killed this pastor who—" She blushes. "You *know.* Anyhow. She killed him with a butcher knife. She's going to real prison when she gets old enough."

"Good for her," I say, with considerably more boldness than I feel.

I look over at Wren, bent over whatever Harry Potter book she's reading now, and try to imagine her doing anything at all, let alone killing someone.

"Look. I'm not going to be in a family with anyone, okay?"

"Good," Jessica says. "Because it's against the rules. But some people—like Maria and them—do it anyway and they get away with it until something bad happens, which it always does. Fighting or getting caught in each other's rooms or in the bathroom together. Then there's trouble, which believe me you do not want to get yourself into. Those Black girls?" she continues. "They're one, too."

"Right," I say. "I know."

They're more like abandoned siblings in a story book, though. Lauvette is clearly in charge, but she acts more like a big sister than a mom— so sure that she's cooler and smarter and more beautiful than the other girls that she doesn't even need to scare them or make them feel bad.

"Baby," Lauvette will say to Kenyae or Jasmine, "get them to change the channel from that white-ass show." Or, "Sistah, get that Monopoly board from the shelf. I'm gonna win me some *property.*"

It might be nice to be in a family like that, I think. It's probably a good thing they'd never let me in.

Although the best thing of all would be to spend every minute in my room, sleeping. I'm exhausted, and I've barely been here a week. All the rules to keep track of, stupid tests, orientation sessions so colossally boring that it's impossible to keep my eyes open—and when I nod off for one single second there's a custody officer right there in my face. Plus, the worry about what Electra is going to mutter under her breath and whether I'll be able to keep from laughing at it or be guilty by association.

And forget napping in the day room: eyes open, feet on the floor at all times. You can read or play board games or watch whatever inane show is on TV. You can do homework, chat quietly with a friend. Praying is allowed; you can close your eyes for that. You can also fold your hands in your lap, close your eyes, and fake-pray. The trouble is, fake-praying makes me fall asleep, too. Jessica taps me awake, saving me from a demerit, but also further convincing herself that she's my personal Wabash Valley Juvenile Correctional Facility behavioral consultant and BFF.

"The thing is," she says now, "honestly, even if families weren't against the rules, they're disgusting. You can see how some girls act like boys. Why would they do that? And other girls let them boss them around like they would a boyfriend. Some act like they're babies—honestly, they talk in baby talk to the ones who decide to be the moms. I have my own family, thank you very much. I have my own beautiful little boy—and who would want to be in a family made up of people who ended up in a place like this, anyway? Also, it's a sin. Families with only girls in them? The Bible says that's wrong."

That is such bullshit, I want to say—*should* say because 1) that evangelical crap goes against everything I believe and, 2) maybe Jessica would decide she didn't want to be my friend if she knew what I think about God. But I don't want anyone to know what I believe about anything, and in the day room, someone is always listening.

"Jesus, chill," I say. "I *said*, I don't want to be in a family. Any. Family. Like, not even my own. So, can we please change the subject?"

From the look on Jessica's face, you'd think I just said I had a terminal disease. "Everybody needs a family," she says. "If your family—if someone in your family, you know, hurts you, you can be in mine. My real family, I mean. You could be Damien's aunt: Aunt Grace. Wouldn't that be so great? You don't actually have to be related to be an aunt, you know? You can just decide. My mom has this friend, Cara, her best friend, and I always called her Aunt Cara when I was little. She's so, so sweet—she's always buying presents for Damien, stuffed animals and books of Bible stories and the cutest little outfits, once she even came here with my mom. We can be like that, Grace," she says. "When we get out, me and Damien could come up to visit you in Indianapolis and, you know, do things. But until then we need to stick together, stay away from trouble, that's what Pastor Dean says—not the stick together part because he doesn't know you, not yet, but it would be so great if you came to fellowship with me. You'd like him. He's not old; he's really cool. Anyway. He always says, 'There's a *lot* of trouble in this place, but if you give your heart to Jesus, He won't let it find you.'"

It's pointless to argue with Jessica. To engage in any way would just egg her on. And it would only confuse her to point out the irony in the fact that—despite her righteous determination not to break the rules, despite her Christian convictions about girls loving girls—she seems to have appointed herself my prison mom.

The Red Suitcase

Nana bought me a red suitcase when my dad moved out. It had Ariel on it, my favorite Disney princess, and wheels so I didn't have to carry it. I loved that suitcase. I played "vacation" with it, putting clothes and toys in it, then rolled it around the house, all the while talking to my stuffed animals about what we would do when we got to Disneyworld. Sometimes I pretended the suitcase was a dog and took it for a walk around the yard.

But the suitcase made me sad when my mom packed it for me to take to my dad's new apartment. I didn't like it there, even though my dad always had special treats when I went, Skittles and caramel corn. And when I woke up on Saturday morning on the living room couch that turned into a bed, my dad would bring donuts and orange juice on a tray and we'd watched cartoons together.

I didn't like him being there instead of home. That was the problem with the apartment. He wouldn't be coming home; he said he couldn't because this was his home now. But I didn't understand why. I also didn't understand why his new home had hardly any room for me. There was barely any furniture. Just the couch and television in the living room, a bed in his bedroom, shelves with blue plastic bins for his clothes—and two empty ones to put my clothes, books, and toys in when I visited. Two lone stools at the kitchen counter for eating dinner.

The good thing was, we did things together when I stayed there. We went to the Children's Museum, where they had dinosaurs and a whole row of dollhouse rooms—beautiful rooms with tiny, perfect chairs and tables and rugs and dishes that I loved to look at. He took me swimming in the warm weather and ice-skating when it was cold. Once we went to a drive-in movie theater, where we sat in the car and watched Monsters, Inc on the big screen outside.

My favorite place was the zoo, especially the meerkats with their pointy faces and big round eyes, and watching the elephants get their baths. I liked riding the train that went through the Africa part of the zoo. Sometimes we rode it two—or even three—times.

When we got on, my dad would always say, "Keep your eyes out for the squirrel exhibit, Grace. I don't know why we can't ever find the squirrel exhibit."

"Daaad," I'd say. "Squirrels aren't in zoos."

"What?" he'd say back. "They're not? That's not fair!"

Then we'd laugh. We thought it was so funny.

One day, just after I started second grade, his friend, Marlys, came with us. She said, "You're so pretty," when he introduced us and that made me happy. But she thought the meerkats were creepy; she didn't want to wait to see the elephants get their baths. And she thought my dad really *was* looking for a squirrel exhibit.

"Bob, why in the world would there be squirrels in a zoo?" she asked. "People don't even like squirrels in the wild, they're always trying to get rid of them."

I liked squirrels a lot. I liked how busy they were, and I thought it was amazing how they could jump from branch to branch and walk along wires way up in the sky. And it was so cute how they nibbled nuts they held in their little hands.

But Marlys looked mad, so I didn't say so.

"Did you like Marlys?" my dad asked after we dropped her off at her house.

I knew he wanted me to like her, so I pretended I did.

He beamed and gave me a big hug. "I just knew you would," he said. "And guess what? She's going to be your other mom. We're going to get married. You'll have *two* families now."

But Marlys didn't want to be in a family with me, which I figured out because it turned out she had two faces: one for when she was alone with me and one for when my dad was there. She had two voices to go along with them. If we were all together and I did something bad, like forget to say please and thank you or not pick up my toys, Marlys's face would look sad and she'd use her fake-sweet voice to say, "I know these things aren't so important to your mom, Grace, but your dad and I want you to have good manners and to learn how to take care of your things, so when you're at our house you need to go by our rules—and those rules are made to teach you how to be a person other people will want to be with."

But if I did something wrong when my dad wasn't with us, her face looked like a thundercloud. Her eyes flashed, her jaw clenched, and she yelled at me and said I was a bad, stupid, selfish girl. That she was going to talk to my dad about sending me back to my mom's house for good this time if I kept on the way I was. She said she didn't know why in the world he loved me like he did, why he kept on taking care of me and forgiving me and making excuses for me when anyone could see that my mom and I were two peas in a pod, both of us determined to make our lives miserable.

One time she forgot my dad was there and had to squeeze out fake tears and pretend she was sorry. "I love Grace," she said. "I try so hard, but can't you see it's impossible when her mom does everything she possibly can to poison her against me?"

Then she started crying and my dad said, "Come on now, Grace. Look what you've done, you've made Marlys cry. Can't you *try* to be a better girl for her?"

Recreation

Captain Donnelly is the supervisor of the Shape Up Zone: short, stocky, strong, no-nonsense, bristling with energy. Clipboard under one arm, silver whistle on a chain around her neck. She welcomes Electra and me to the Shape Up Zone orientation session, then nods toward the makeshift sign on the wall behind her desk. Two words typed in a huge font and mounted on foam core:

Recreation = Re-Creation

"Recreation," she says. "The Shape Up Zone is a place where you take a break from your schoolwork and chores to enjoy the benefits exercise brings to your mind and body.

"But—" Captain Donnelly regards both of us with hard eyes, fingering her whistle. "What we're really in the business of here at Wabash Valley is *re*-creation. It is our goal to, literally, return you to the world re-created—ready to take on the challenge of living a healthy, productive life."

"Young Frankenstein: female offender version," Electra murmurs.

Thank God Captain Donnelly just blathers on.

"In case you are wondering why I am called Captain, I was a captain in the United States Army: three tours, Afghanistan. I know the power of discipline. I know the power of strength."

I can feel Electra beside me, bristling with energy herself, but I don't dare look at her. It's more than enough just to keep the rules straight and the shit that's been bubbling up ever since I got here at bay. Jack. My parents' divorce. Ancient fucking history. Why won't it stay that way? The last thing I need is new shit to deal with because of Electra.

"Physical activity, building a healthy relationship with your body, is required," Captain Donnelly says. "Every girl has a PAP, a Physical Activity Program, and you are here today to explore the opportunities the Shape Up Zone has to offer."

The facility is the size of several gyms—a basketball court, a volleyball court, ping pong tables, and a running track around the perimeter. There are basketballs and volleyballs on a long shelf, ping pong balls and paddles in plastic containers, jump ropes hanging on a hook. There's a jumble of blue jerseys in a laundry basket. More motivational posters impossible to avoid, these versions decorated with every kind of ball you could imagine.

Life Is Not a Spectator Sport. Get in the Game.

Don't Count the Days. Let the Days Count.

Without a Goal You Can't Score.

Be a Winner, Not a Whiner.

"When you enter," Captain Donnelly says, "you sign in, request an activity, then go to the locker room to change into your regulation gym shorts and T-shirt. Five minutes for that, tops. A sweatshirt may be worn in colder weather, but if you put on a sweatshirt you must wear it for the entire recreation period—"

"Why can't you take it off if you get too hot?" Electra asks.

"Because that is the rule," Captain Donnelly responds. "You are issued a towel, which must be checked in at the end of your session." She goes on, listing. "There is no talking in the Shape Up Zone, except for what's necessary for game play. Absolutely. No. Cursing. You must ask permission of one of the student proctors to use the water fountain."

There are girls whose work detail is monitoring the group to see that rules are followed and to address any concerns or requests. Five of them, each wearing a red tee-shirt with PROCTOR in white letters, observing us from their posts around the Shape Up Zone.

"You will do what the proctors tell you to do," Captain Donnelly says. "You do *not* want them to have to ask me to intervene."

There are maybe twenty other girls in the facility now: tall, strong, fierce girls running up and down the basketball court, gleaming with sweat; tense; wiry girls playing ping pong; girls with slumped shoulders, heads down, trudging around the track like they're on a death march; fat red-faced girls, struggling to keep moving at all. One girl, just one, running—flying, really—arms pumping, an otherworldly expression on her face.

There's no sound but the thud of basketballs, the screech of sneakers on the gym floor, the thwock of ping pong balls on the table, the rhythmic pounding of shoes on the track. The occasional burst of laughter.

There is no sitting around in the Shape Up Zone.

There Are No Excuses.

"Waiting is walking," Captain Donnelly says. "If you sign up for an activity that is full, you will walk—or run, if you prefer—the perimeter of the Shape Up Zone until that activity becomes available to you. You're not feeling well? Do you think my lady soldiers were excused from battle if they didn't feel well, when they had their periods? They were not. They marched, they fought, they exercised to stay in shape. And that is how I run things here. As a matter of fact, joining the military, receiving the kind of training you need to lead a good, wholesome life, is an excellent option upon release from this facility and I want you to be fully prepared should you make that choice."

She consults her clipboard. "Questions?"

"No, ma'am," I say.

"No, ma'am," Electra echoes.

Captain Donnelly nods at Officer Snap, who gestures for us to fall in line behind her. We exit the Shape Up Zone, hands behind our backs, into a perfect autumn afternoon that makes me think of skipping school not long after I met Kyle, making out in a secluded place along the riverbank, red and gold leaves drifting down on us like gentle rain. A time that feels more like a movie than something that happened in my life.

The Girls of Cottage Five

Oh, God. There's Jessica again. She gives a little wave, tucks in front of me in the breakfast line. "Good morning," she whispers. I ignore her and continue to ignore her in the cafeteria, where she wolfs down her runny scrambled eggs and half-cooked bacon, all the while watching me with a hopeful expression, pleading without words, *please be my friend*.

But I'm done with being friends with girls—any girls. I was done before I messed up bad enough to land me here. It was because of Zoe, who decided in seventh grade that she wanted to be best friends with Monica instead of me. In fact, Zoe didn't want to be friends with me at all—which was the beginning of my long spiral downward that finally stopped when I met Kyle.

"Let it go," he told me, when I tried to explain how badly Zoe hurt me. "You're way prettier and smarter than Zoe. And Monica—she's a bitch. Why do you care about either one of them? Why do you care about anyone at all when we have each other?"

He was right about needing to let it go, of course. But I still felt sad every time I saw Zoe. I still sometimes longed to go backward in time to when it was just the two of us playing Barbies or My Little Pony in Zoe's pink bedroom, Zoe's mom always bringing us apple juice and a bowl of goldfish crackers on a tray the exact minute we got hungry.

The truth is, I never really got over losing Zoe. I'm not sure I ever will—but I don't dare think about her now. I'm up to my ears with things to be sad about, up to my ears remembering every single rule here, up to my ears trying to make sure the instructors and custody officers know that Electra and I are not one bit alike. Which isn't easy.

Today, for example, after Officer Martin's lecture on Staying Sexually Safe, Electra glanced at me, raised her hand, and asked the instructor in a concerned voice, "Is it true that a girl in Cottage Five has AIDS?"

"No!" the instructor said. "Nobody here has AIDS. That is not something you need to worry about."

"Okay. But, like, I heard it from a couple of different people," Electra said. "Grace, you're in Cottage Five, aren't you? Have you heard anything about it?"

I felt myself flush, felt the instructor's eyes on me.

"No," I mumbled.

"Are you sure?" Electra asked. "Because we deserve to know if—"

"Enough," the instructor said. "I promise, you are perfectly safe here. You both are."

"Safe from *AIDS*," Electra said to me, when we were out of earshot. "Not so much from anything else. And I did hear it, by the way. In the cafeteria. People were really freaked out. Well done."

"I was going to tell you."

"No, you weren't." Electra grinned. "Anyway, you didn't need to. I'm psychic, I knew you'd take my advice. I know all."

Was she joking? I couldn't tell.

Which made me think about Zoe again, how I'd missed every signal when Zoe invited me to come to Monica's church's sleepover camp with them the summer after sixth grade. Yes! I said, thrilled because I thought the invitation meant Zoe had finally convinced Monica that we could be three friends together. I couldn't wait.

But the day we left for camp, Zoe and Monica chose two seats together on the bus, and the only seat left was at the back of the bus, next to a kid I later found out was nicknamed Bible Nerd.

"Are you saved?" he asked two seconds after I sat down.

"From *what?*"

He gave me a look, like he felt sorry for me, and shrank away like I had some dreaded disease. I didn't care. I was pretty sure I'd start crying if I had to talk to anyone, even a creep like him.

It was hot and airless on the bus. My face felt like it was burning, sweat trickled down my spine. There was a lot of singing, which made my head hurt, and I couldn't read because the bus swaying back and forth was giving me motion sickness. I had to close my eyes to keep from feeling nauseous. So, I just sat there next to Bible Nerd, praying—even though I didn't believe in God anymore—that I wouldn't throw up.

The camp turned out to be a decrepit old farm. The camp director, Pastor Brad, lived in the ramshackle farmhouse with his family. The barn, which still smelled faintly of animals, had been made into a dining hall and rec center, and dorms lined with bunk beds on either side, one for boys and one for girls. There was a weedy lake, some scrubby woods, a big fire pit. And, of course, a camp church—really just a thatched shelter with wooden benches instead of pews and a gargantuan rock with the top shaved off for the pulpit.

"This place is gross," Monica said to me when we got off the bus—like it was my fault—and she and Zoe flounced off, leaving me standing all alone. They chose bunks together, and by the time I got to the dorm there were none left near them. At lunch they found a table with only two seats available. And when Zoe was made captain for a volleyball game later that day, she didn't choose me. The two of them huddled together under one blanket at the evening campfire.

Had they planned this? Had Monica said to Zoe, "It's the only way Grace is going to *get* that you don't want to be friends with her anymore?" Or had it just been an unspoken impulse when they got on the bus this morning?

Either way, I got it now.

I avoided them, searched out quiet places where I could sit by myself and pretend to be praying. But Pastor Brad had some kind of radar for loneliness. Every time he saw me alone, he'd come over to me, arms outstretched, and I'd have to let him hug me. Then he'd drag me over to some group that seemed to be having fun, but then stopped having fun when Pastor Brad presented me to them. They weren't mean kids, some made lame attempts to be friendly, but all I wanted was for the endless week to be over.

Sometimes I felt like I was disappearing, turning into gray fog among the laughter, the constant chatter, the rise and fall of Pastor Brad's voice, preaching, the odd rhythms of Bible verses being recited. When Saturday finally came, I was the first one on the bus. I chose a seat all the way in the back and choosing felt like a small triumph.

But the next time I saw Zoe and Monica, on the first day of seventh grade, and they ignored me, I had to lean against the locker bay to keep myself from sliding to the floor and curling into a black ball of grief.

Until Kyle, I avoided people my own age.

Until Kyle—and look where that got me.

The very thought of him doubles my resolve to keep my distance from Electra, cut off Jessica's attempts to befriend me, and keep an eye on the other girls in Cottage Five, for good measure—

Destiny, with her buzz cut and butch swagger, scowling and smirking. Except with Kaylie, her girlfriend—a whiny, blond, blue-eyed stick of a girl, who Destiny is always trying to please.

Maria, the matriarch; Amber, Adrienne, and Bree, her devoted daughters.

The self-proclaimed African Queens: Kenyae, Jasmine, Lauvette.

Wren, the murderer—who reads.

THREE

Board Game

I used to play Candy Land with my dad when I was really little. We'd pretend-float along the board on ice cream floats, with an orange Creamsicle for shade, pluck chocolate from the gingerbread man tree—and eventually make it to the cozy cottage with its peppermint stick fence, ice cream cone flowers, and round green Lifesaver window. A sign next to its candy bar steps said, "Home Sweet Home."

I got so excited I could barely sit still if I got the green square right at the beginning because it meant I got to zoom my blue gingerbread man (I always picked the blue one) up the Rainbow Trail, way ahead of my dad's red one. Once, the very first card I pulled was the peanut brittle card and—boom—I was halfway to winning already. If I picked a card that said I had to go backward on the board my dad let me pick another and another until I picked one that let me go forward. If I got too far behind, he'd skip turns so I could catch up and pass him and win. It made my mom furious.

"Children need to play by the rules," she'd say.

But my dad did it anyway.

"You know," Electra said one day, "being in this fucking place is a whole lot like playing a board game. Each square's a day in your sentence and you're the red or blue or yellow or green plastic gingerbread man—"

"Candyland!" I say. "Best game ever."

Electra raises her hand for a high-five, and I slap it.

"No Gum Drop Mountains, though," I say. "Or Peppermint Stick Forest."

"Ha! And forget the Rainbow Trail. *That's* not allowed."

I burst out laughing just as Officer Snap returns, only half-recovering with a fake cough. But she just gives us the evil eye and jerks her thumb for us to follow her.

"Back to the board," Electra mouths as we move on to the next square.

I can't stop seeing a game board in my head: a map of Wabash Valley and me, a game piece moving through Lollipop Woods and Molasses Swamps of idiotic programs, with their idiotic rewards and demerits.

Start at GO in your newbie orange jump suit. Then proceed through:

"Cage Your Rage." *Move backward when anger simmers over.*

"Thinking for a Change." *Move forward with reports that reflect cognitive restructuring of the crappy values that got you here, or backwards if you fuck up.*

"Voices." *Stay stuck in one place for several turns until you can fake Celebrate Yourself.*

Shortcut through "Gang Realities in Our World." (Because you are not a gang member.)

Hover in place at "Purposeful Living." (Until you suck it up and start going to chapel to enhance your moral, spiritual, and character development.)

Endure "Stay Sharp Substance Abuse Program." (Because it's assumed that anybody who gets in this place is bound to have a problem with drugs or alcohol or both. But whatever you do, don't ask why the drugs they give you every night to knock you out are perfectly OK.)

Proceed without smirking through the ten lame metaphors of "Why Try" (including "reality ride," "tearing off your label," "jumping hurdles," "get plugged in," and "you can see over the wall), *convincing your counselor that you are gaining* "New Social and Coping Skills to Break Old Behavior Patterns and Achieve Opportunity, Freedom, and Self-Respect" (so you don't blow it when you get the hell out of this place).

Shortcut through "Sexual Abuse Recovery." (Because nobody knows about Jack.)

Appear appropriately enthused about winning Perks for Good Behavior, which include:

- Proctor: Boss fellow inmates around and bust them for breaking the rules.
- Teacher's assistant: Do the teacher's work and maybe get a better grade.
- Behavior Review Panel member: Judge fellow inmates and decide on their punishment for small, stupid infractions that the staff doesn't really care about.
- PAWS: Train abandoned dogs to be worthy of a Forever Family (which is not you).
- Peer Tutor: Help fellow inmates with their homework, but probably actually do it for them.

"Wahoo!" Electra muttered at the end of the Perks for Good Behavior session. "Who wouldn't want to be good?"

Operation

My dad left the Candy Land game behind when he went to live with Marlys, and my mom didn't like to play board games. So, it just sat there on a shelf in my bedroom until, once, Jack was visiting and played with me—

until Aunt Marjorie got irritated and called in a fake-sweet voice, "Jack, come play with the adults now." So, he bought Candy Land for Jack Camp, so we could play as much as we wanted to.

We played Twister, too, which made me laugh when we got all tangled up together on the big plastic sheet spread out on the floor. Then Jack would tickle me, and I'd laugh even harder.

But our favorite game was Operation, which he gave me for my eighth birthday to help me learn the parts of the body. The game board was just a drawing of a goofy-looking guy, Sam, wearing boxer shorts with hearts on them, with little holes all over him to put his ailments in (things that hurt him, Jack explained when I said I didn't know what 'ailments' meant). You took turns trying to get the ailments out with special tweezers, trying not to touch the metal edge of the ailment hole because a buzzer sounded, Sam's nose lit up red, and you lost your next turn. There was an Adam's apple in his neck, a wrench in his ankle, a pail of water on one knee, a little horse on his leg, a wishbone on his chest, a heart with a crack through it on the other, a butterfly on his stomach.

I got butterflies in my stomach when we finished playing Operation with Sam and Jack said it was my turn to be the patient.

"Don't move a single muscle," he'd say.

And I'd lie very still on the floor with my shorts on, like Sam, and Jack would put the game pieces on my body very carefully so they wouldn't fall off—just barely touching me with the tips of his fingers. He'd say the name of each one, and I would say the definition—which he said was good for my vocabulary.

Wrenched ankle means sprained ankle.

The Adam's apple is cartilage surrounding the larynx.

Water on the knee is fluid gathering around the knee joint.

A Charlie Horse is a sudden spasm in the leg or foot.

Wish bone is the nickname for the *furcula*, a bone found in birds and some other animals.

"Good Girl," Jack would say when I named them all correctly.

I had butterflies in my stomach when he used the tweezers to take the game pieces off of my body, too. He'd try not to touch my skin with them, but sometimes he couldn't help it. When that happened, he made a buzzing sound through his teeth that made me giggle, which sometimes made the other game pieces slide off.

Jack would say, "Grace! Grace! Grace!"—and pull me over his knee and pretend-spank me, which made me giggle more.

I swear to God, I would kill him if I thought I could get away with it—like Wren did to the pastor who molested her. But taking the chance, maybe blowing it isn't worth ending up like Wren—who doesn't even have a game piece to move, no program whose steps will lead her through the locked gates, home.

Your Health and Well Being

It wasn't like I hadn't noticed Kyle: his muscular, swimmer's build, his square jaw, the straw-colored hair that flopped across his forehead. That wicked, lopsided grin. How every single day he dashed into Your Health and Well Being just before the bell and slid into his seat behind me—knees bent, arms out, like a surfer. The class met the last period of the day. Most people slept or sat like zombies through the teacher's lame Power Points. Kyle was one of the sleepers. I knew by the sound of his breathing.

He hated the class, he told me. It pissed him off. Why should you have to do boring, stupid shit just because some asshat decided?

He said, "Rules are for people with no imagination."

This was after he followed me out of class one day, caught my arm, and said, "Hey. You want to go get coffee?"

"Me?" *Jesus.* I sounded like Minnie Mouse.

"Yeah, you," he said.

Was this some kind of joke, I wondered? Worse, a dare? Boys never noticed me.

"Hey!" Kyle said. "Earth to Grace. You clearly need caffeine. So, come on. Let's do it."

The next thing I knew, we were in his silver Jeep heading for the local coffeehouse, Kyle bobbing to a playlist of everything from heavy metal to pop to hip-hop on the car stereo—which, thankfully, made conversation impossible. When we got there, he ordered three double espressos, then raised his hand when I reached for my backpack and said, "Boyfriend always pays."

He drank the first espresso in a single gulp the moment the barista put it on the counter, then carried the others to an open table and set one of them before me. I usually ordered a caramel macchiato or maybe pumpkin spice in season—with extra whipped cream to cut the bitterness—but I picked up the double espresso and drank it down in a gulp just like Kyle had.

"Well done," he said.

I laughed, which totally shocked me; I'd never in my life laughed with a boy. Almost two hours—along with two more espressos and a shared chocolate chip scone—passed before I remembered that I was staying at my dad's house that night and Marlys would grill me if I got there too much later than usual.

"I get it," Kyle said. "Never alert a stepmother to anything that matters."

"You have a stepmother, too?"

"Nah. Just the usual kind. Same principle applies." He put his iPhone on the table, slid it toward me. "Put your number in," he said, "then give me yours and I'll put mine in it."

My hand-me-down Samsung was turned off, zipped into a pocket of my backpack. Thanks to Marlys, it had no text service and just enough calling minutes to cover family logistics and any kind of emergency that might pop up. Usually not a problem since there was nobody I wanted to call or text, no big deal, and who was going to call or text *me?*

Kyle looked at me. "You don't *have* a cell?"

"Yeah, I do. But I'm only allowed to use it for family stuff."

"Dude. That is crazy wrong."

It was also crazy wrong that I had to take the bus to school, he said. He'd pick me up the next morning—at the bus stop, the same place he dropped me off after coffee.

"Group project," I said, when Marlys asked where I'd been.

My bedroom was really the guest room and, that evening, it felt less like my own than ever. I felt less like myself than ever. I sat on the bed with its hideous floral duvet, wondering what, exactly, had happened with Kyle and what I was supposed to do about this weird sensation I had—a kind of tickling heat at the core of me—when he leaned over and kissed me just before I got out of the car.

"Boyfriend always pays," he'd said when we got coffee.

He didn't even know me.

I barely slept that night, running it all through my mind. It scared me a little: how I felt. And what if I got to the bus stop in the morning and Kyle was there with a bunch of his friends, laughing as he hit the gas and sped away. Zoe and Monica would find out—Monica smiling her superior smile, rolling her eyes at the news.

"Oh, please," she'd say. "And Grace thought he was *serious?*"

But there he was the next morning, waiting a few houses down from where kids gathered for the bus. When I slid into the front seat, he handed me an iPhone box. "It's all set up," he said. "Unlimited everything. I put my number in your favorites."

"You can't give me an iPhone," I said.

"Yeah," he said. "I can. I just did. And in case you're worried about your parents finding out, I got you a new number. You can keep the old phone for calling them."

"But—"

"Hold it," he said. "Last night, after I dropped you off, didn't you wonder if I would've texted you if you had a decent phone?"

Damn. I could feel myself blushing.

He grinned. "FYI: I would have. Thus, I went to the Apple store so I could. Open it."

I did. When I touched the screen, a text message floated on blue sky and clouds: *"Amazing Grace! Welcome to Kyle-World."*

Kyle took it from my hand, tapped the camera, and leaned in close to me. "Smile." He snapped a selfie of the two of us, pushed some buttons, and *voila*! We were the wallpaper. "Look at you. You're beautiful," he said.

I was. I had never in my whole life looked like that.

I used to be so amused by my classmates, with their phones tucked in open backpacks at their feet, balanced on their thighs. Their ringers were turned off, but the phones were constantly lighting up or vibrating with notifications for texts or Snapchat or Instagram, and I'd watch their hands creep to their phones, then tap the screen for a quick read. Sometimes, eyes front, even type a response.

What was so important it couldn't wait, I wondered.

Now I knew. I was like everyone else now, one eye on the teacher, the other on the phone balanced on my thigh, waiting for the rush of connection when the dark screen flickered, stealthily tapping my password so I could read the whole message, text a response.

Sometimes Kyle sent hilarious photos and I had to clench my jaw not to laugh. He sent emojis, favoring weird custom variations of the smiley face: like with gritted teeth or marijuana leaves for eyeballs. Once, when I texted him to say I'd gotten an A on my chemistry test, he texted back an emoji of Einstein with his tongue stuck out.

At home, I kept the phone in the front pocket of my backpack, the ringer off, the notifications disabled. I took quick peeks at it while I did my homework but didn't actually take it out until I was sure my parents had gone to bed. Then Kyle and I would text for hours. It was delicious—lying in bed, moonlight falling in through the window, feeling as if he were right there with me.

Stop, I tell myself now, remembering this. *Kyle is not good for you. You'd never in a million years have gotten into so much trouble if you hadn't met him.*

I swear. If there's one thing I'm going to do while I'm in this shithole, it's Stop Loving Kyle. But how am I supposed to do that when I can't stop missing him? Can't stop hearing his voice? Sometimes, sleepless, I lie on my thin mattress, my thumbs moving, texting onto my bent knees as if the words might actually reach him.

Tree House Person

Jessica's questions are never-ending. "When's your birthday?" "What music do you like? What's your favorite food? Do you have any brothers or sisters?" She's like a fly buzzing. Sometimes I have to hold my hands in my lap to keep from swatting at her.

"What did you think about the tests?" she asks the second I get to the day room after a long afternoon of testing. "Didn't you love the tree/house/person one? Didn't you think it was cool? I drew this big house, the house me and Damien are going to live in someday. A whole super-big house all to ourselves except my mom can live there if she wants and maybe my husband if I find the right guy, you know, a really nice person with a good job, someone who loves me and Damien to death, and I decide to want to get married. There might be some other kids, too, if that happens," she says. "A little girl, for sure.

"Oh, and my tree! With a tree house for Damien in it, nice and shady underneath so I can sit there while he plays. Damien was my person. But I couldn't draw him right, you know? So that part kind of made me sad because I can see him perfectly inside my head and, I mean, if I can see him so good why can't I draw him?"

"It's okay if he didn't look exactly right," I say. "The test wasn't about being an artist."

Why tell her I thought the tree/house/person test was stupid? That all the tests they made us take were stupid. I mean, really. The depression inventory, the personal assessment inventory, the anxiety inventory—and, my personal favorite, the hopelessness scale.

All made further annoying because, trapped in the claustrophobic testing room, I heard Kyle's voice clear as a bell. "The trick to those tests shrinks give you," he said, "is to figure out what they expect you to answer and choose that. They think they're God, but they're really suckers. It's a game just like everything else: they think winning is solving you, like you're some kind of puzzle. So, you let them think they solved you, then collect whatever your parents promised they'd give you if you shaped your ass up— then fake it until they stop paying attention to you again. That's how I got the Jeep."

He'd been so smug about it. Then incredulous when I told him my parents took things *away* when I did something wrong: television privileges, weekend visits with Briony.

"That's fucked," he said.

Still, it was sweet how pissed off it made him, how completely incomprehensible it was to him that my parents didn't see that bad behavior was a sign of unhappiness, that they didn't love me enough to do anything, give me anything to make me feel better.

"Fuck them," he said. "Fuck being who they want you to be." He put his arms around me and said, "Dude, it's you and me. You and me, forever."

Right, I think. And now he's in that school for messed up rich kids, being the soulful, sensitive, peace-loving person he needs to be to rack up whatever points he needs to go home. Not locked up, not lining up for nauseating, inedible meals, not surrounded by thugs or meth heads—rich kids like expensive drugs. It made me so mad I started shaking and couldn't stop. Then a tsunami of anxiety hit me and I couldn't breathe.

I was alone in the testing room when it happened, a room not much bigger than the closet I used to hide in at Jack's house. There was a guard outside the door, but he couldn't see me unless he bothered to stand up and look through the webbed window, which was unlikely because, as far as I could tell, nobody here did more than they absolutely had to do. The truth is, I was glad of it. The last thing I wanted was for word to get out that I could be freaked out by…anything.

I got myself calmed down and saw, as much as I hated to admit it, Kyle probably wasn't wrong. Figure out what they want you to say and say that. So, I drew a generic house, a generic tree, a generic person—and answered the questions in the most possible suck-up way.

Who lives here? *A family.*

Are the occupants happy? *Sometimes yes, sometimes no.*

What goes on inside the house? *Day to day things: cooking, cleaning, watching TV.*

What's it like at night? *Quiet.*

Do people visit the house? *Sometimes.*

Who? *Friends. Family. Neighbors.*

What kind of tree is this? *Maple.*

How old is the tree? *I don't know. Old.*

Has anyone ever tried to cut it down? *No.*

What season is it? *Spring.*

What else grows nearby? *More trees.*

Who waters this tree? *Rain.*

Who is the person? *A girl.*

How old is the person? *Ten.*

What does she like and dislike doing? *She likes reading, she dislikes chores.*

Has anyone tried to hurt her? *No.*

Who looks out for her? *Her parents.*

"Tell me about them." Kyle asked me one afternoon. "Your parents. You can tell me."

And I did. But I didn't tell him about Jack because I was afraid he might kill him—or worse, blame or judge me. Not that I didn't want Jack dead, I did. But if Kyle killed him and got caught even his parents couldn't keep him from going to prison and then I'd have no one.

Clearly a wasted opportunity, I see now, because taking up with him turned out to be the biggest mistake I ever made. Jack's still alive, *I'm* the one in prison, and my parents love me even less than they did before I met Kyle.

A Series of Unfortunate Events

"You are going to prison, Grace," Marlys said. "Not some School for Troubled Rich Kids like your boyfriend, where they'll coddle you and let you keep believing that everything bad that ever happened to you is someone else's fault. I hope you'll use this time you've been given to think hard about how you ended up in this mess."

"*A Series of Unfortunate Events: The Slippery Slope*," I said.

"You think it's funny," Marlys said. "You think I don't know you read those dreadful books to your sister when I've forbidden them? Well, think again. And while you're at it, you might consider the fact that, while you're convinced all the reprehensible things you've done have somehow made you an adult, the law still regards you as a juvenile—and that means they can keep you locked up as long as they want to. You know, Grace, you're going to have to jump through their hoops to earn back your freedom—and I think we all know you're not good at hoops."

I'd have strangled Marlys if I could. Or better yet, put her in a room with Jack, let him do to Marlys what he did to me and then strangle her. Oh, and let my dad watch. No point involving my mom because she'd be texting someone or a call would come in that she absolutely had to take and she'd get distracted.

In fact, she was texting that very moment, taking a break from berating my dad for how badly I turned out. How she had to bear the burden of raising me virtually alone. And I was always so difficult, even when I was little. Blah, blah, blah.

We were in a windowless beige conference room with uncomfortable plastic furniture, where we'd been deposited to wait until I was taken away.

Marlys went on, now reassuring my dad that he was in no way responsible for my being a convicted thief. "You did everything you could for her," she said. "We both did. And look at her! Look at your daughter, Bob. That smirk on her face. She's glad this is hurting you so much."

He just sat there, waiting for it to be over.

Marlys sighed. "The sad truth is that all any of us can do for her now is pray—"

"*Really?*" I said. "And what, exactly, will you be praying for? That I'll go to jail and come out just like you? Because, you know, I'd prefer the electric chair."

Marlys gasped. Her hands flew to her face.

"Sweetheart," Grace's father said—to *Marlys*. He looked like he was about to cry.

"Grace, please—"

"Don't even go there," I said to him. "Don't even *talk* to me until you get some balls and tell that bitch that what happens to me is none of her fucking business. It never has been."

Then he did start crying, which made my mom look up from her phone and roll her eyes. Marlys cast her a murderous glance.

The two of them were like cats with their claws out. I loved when that happened and waited for the blow-up. But just then the state cop appeared. He cuffed me, put the shackles on my legs, and held his hand out to help me from the chair.

"Is there anything you'd like to say to your parents before we go?"

"No," I said. "Not a goddamn thing. Just please get me away from them."

Mental Health

The morning after the last test, Officer Snap calls for me at Cottage Five and I follow her into the unseasonably sweltering morning. The one maple tree in the center of the campus, imprisoned by crisscrossing sidewalks, has turned almost completely red—but it's as hot as it was the day I got here and, suddenly, it's as if no time has passed at all and I'm pissed all over again that I'd been cuffed in the back seat of the police car all the way from Indianapolis. Pissed that I could hardly move because the seatbelt was so tight, that the hot sun coming through the window burned my face and made me nauseous. The twists and turns in the road, the way the landscape blurred as we sped along had made it worse, the little hills I was sure the cop took too quickly to make my stomach roll each time. They made me think of Jack, how he called them 'oopsy-daisy hills' when I was little and sped up to tickle my tummy because it made me laugh and say, "More! More!" Which also pissed me off—and is still pissing me off, right this second, because I so do not need to be thinking about Jack right now and he's been floating to the surface ever since I got here.

"Move it, Lowery. No stopping."

I jolt forward, almost tripping. I didn't even know I had stopped.

Officer Snap delivers me to the office of an older lady with gray, bobbed hair, who crisply dismisses her, as if she doesn't like her any more than I do.

"I'm Dr. Welty," she says. "We're going to work together to help you find the best way to get through your time here and make use of it." She smiles. "I know. Getting through—okay. But actually making use of being here probably seems not so likely at this point."

I'm startled by the sound of her voice. It has the South in it, like Jack's cleaning lady, Belle. Stout, round-faced Belle, who hugged me and was always kind to me and watched me sometimes, as if she knew. The memory of her voice brings back the feel of being wrapped up in her arms, my head against her beating heart, but it also makes me remember all the times I came so close to telling Belle about Jack but never did. Because I was afraid Jack would hurt Belle or fire her and that wouldn't be fair. What Jack did wasn't Belle's fault. Plus, if I told Belle and Belle told my mom, my mom would say I was lying, *always* lied—

I haven't allowed myself to cry not once since I've been here, but now I'm sobbing and can't make myself stop. I'm furious with myself, furious with Dr. Welty, who watches patiently, her eyes kind. What I'd like to do is scratch those eyes out. What good is kindness to me? And make use of my time here? Please. What I want is *out*.

If only I could become my tattoo and make beautiful chaos of this place! Fling my folder in the air and watch all the assessments of who I am scatter everywhere, dump the folders of all the girls with problems Dr. Welty thinks she can solve out of her file cabinet, clear her shelves of the books by fucking know-it-all experts and, most of all, smash the happy family photos arranged so neatly at the edge of her desk.

At least Dr. Welty doesn't say something inane, like, "It's good to cry" when I finally stop and pull myself together. She just hands me a box of tissues and says, "Today I'd just like to ask you some questions, Grace. No worries. Just answer as best you can."

But they're weird questions, unsettling, and harder to lie about.

"Who do you call family?"

"Nobody."

Dr. Welty waits.

"I don't *call* them family," I say. "They don't deserve it."

"Are there people in your life who feel like family, even though you're not related?"

"No."

"Are there people in your actual family you wish you could feel closer to? Or know you could be closer to if it weren't for the others?"

"No."

"If you could change that family, how would you change it?"

"I wouldn't. I'd resign and never see any of them again. Ever."

She doesn't write anything down like other shrinks do, just keeps going. "Do you ever wish you could make a family of people you choose? Can you imagine a group of people, people you may or may not know now but the kind of people with whom you might like to be close?"

"I don't want any kind of family at all."

"In that case, who would you go to if you were sick or in trouble?"

"I'd take care of myself," I say. "I've always done that, anyway."

Dr. Welty pauses, as if she, too, can see the memories this lie triggers. Kyle at his parents' ski house last spring, bringing me tea and toast, sleeping beside me when I felt so horrible, hurt so bad. And Jack, kissing a scrape on my knee to make it feel better—and it did. Tears rush to my eyes; I'm furious at Dr. Welty for making me remember things I want to forget.

But Dr. Welty doesn't push. "What kind of things do you do easily," she goes on. "What are your talents?"

I shrug. *Lie, steal, fuck, agitate*, I'd say if I were as daring as Electra.

Dr. Welty steeples her fingertips, looks at me for a long moment, then continues, "Okay, what things are difficult for you?"

Boredom, self-righteousness, stupid questions.

"Grace?"

I shrug again.

"What do you worry about?"

"I don't. What's the point?"

"You're right about that." A ghost of a smile crosses her face. "Though most of us do."

"Yeah, well—"

She raises her hands, dismissing the question. But, Jesus, she's relentless.

"This, then," she says. "What are you most proud of accomplishing in your life, so far?"

"Truthfully? Making my stepmother's life a living hell."

"So, you're angry," she says.

Duh.

She taps my file. "Your life, in here—it's a mess. But it isn't everything you are. I know that. Do you?"

I couldn't answer the question if I knew, which I don't, because Jack's words are writhing in my throat. *If you tell anyone I'll kill you.*

"Just one more question," Dr. Welty says. "And you don't have to give me an answer now, Grace—or ever. But what I want you to think about before we meet next is: What have you lost?"

Briony

When Jessica asked me if I had brothers or sisters, I said no, and I lied again when I told Dr. Welty there was nobody I called family, because how I feel about Briony is nobody's business but my own. Briony, my nine-year-old sister, who I tried to hate but couldn't because she wouldn't let me. We're actually half-sisters, though Briony always says, "We're *whole* sisters," when anybody calls us that. She's the absolute best thing in my life—well, she was until I got in trouble with Kyle, and Marlys said I was a bad influence and wouldn't let me see her anymore. She told my dad I was no longer welcome in their house and if he wanted to see me, it had to be someplace else.

So, every couple of weeks he took me out to dinner at some crappy place, but all he did was talk about how worried and disappointed both he and Marlys were, how I used to be such a good kid—and what happened? If I asked about Briony, he'd say she's fine, very, very busy with her ballet and horseback riding and schoolwork. Then change the subject. Sometimes I thought he was as afraid of Marlys as I was of Jack.

"He's a pussy," Kyle said. "You should just tell him to fuck off."

When I finally did my dad took me at my word—and that was that.

Sometimes I thought about being with him when I was a little girl, before the divorce, and how my mom always complained that he was spoiling me.

"Believe me, *our* children are going to be better behaved," Marlys said to my dad one time when she was mad at me.

Except they didn't have children of their own yet. I heard my mom tell Aunt Marjorie, "Poor old Bob, Father of the Year. He thinks he can ditch me and take up with somebody willing to put up with his bullshit and have the big, happy family of his dreams and not only does she turn out to be a bitch on wheels, but I've heard she can't get pregnant, so too bad about that."

I felt sorry for Marlys, I wanted to make her feel better, so I told her, "You have me. I can be your girl, too." But she said, "Grace, what in the world are you talking about?"

Then, finally, Marlys was pregnant. My dad took care of her every single minute because her headaches got worse and her back hurt and so did her feet. Then, one weekend I came to stay and my bedroom had been turned into a nursery—pink and white because the baby was going to be a girl. They did it because, when the baby came, she'd be living there all the time and I only visited, my dad told me. My new room was green—a color I didn't like at all. It didn't even have my own bed in it because if guests visited when I was with my mom they would need a bigger one. So, they gave my bed away.

"Could you make my new room yellow—like my room at Nana's was?" I asked.

"Not now," my dad said. "But maybe some time."

I didn't fuss, even though I wanted a yellow room badly. I didn't want to upset him because what if, when the baby was born, he didn't want me anymore? But sometimes I sneaked into the baby's room and sat on the rocking chair with the pink cushion on it and rocked the soft white bunny Marlys had bought for the baby, pretending it was mine. Once I took off its little pink coat—but I was too scared to ever do it again because I almost couldn't get it back on right.

Sometimes in the baby's room, I'd imagine myself small enough to fit into the white crib, my dad pulling the tiny pink quilt up to my chin and me going to sleep and then he'd come back when I woke up and lift me way high into the air like he did when I was little and pretend I was an airplane, yelling, *zoom, zoom, zoom, zoom, zoom.* But pretty soon going in the pink room made me start hating the baby that was coming.

But then Briony came. She was so, so small, with blond hair like baby bird fuzz, waving her arms and legs like she was swimming. She stopped, perfectly still, and looked at me the first time she heard my voice, and when I held out my finger she grabbed it and held on tight and tried to put it in her mouth like she thought it was her own.

And I fell in love with her.

FOUR

Green Bracelet

Ms. Raab, the intake officer snips off my newbie bracelet and replaces it with a green one. "You've done well with orientation," she says. "I hope you'll continue to do so for the rest of your time here."

Electra's bracelet is yellow. She still has some work to do on her attitude, Ms. Raab tells her. If Electra gives a shit, she doesn't show it, and flashes me a grin as we follow Ms. Raab to the dispensary. There, we change from our orange sweats into the regulation khakis, white tee-shirt, and green polo shirt the other girls wear. We're issued an extra set of khaki and green clothes to replace the orange ones we've been wearing since we got here.

They're worn, some patched or stained, smelling faintly of something that can only be traces of the girls who wore them in the past. Ghost clothes, I think, and imagine whatever those girls left of themselves mixing with whatever I'll leave behind myself when I get the fuck out of here. Who were they, I wonder? What did they do, who hurt them so badly that they ended up here?

What did Electra do? We've never talked about it.

"See you around," she says, when a proctor arrives to escort her to her cottage. "Keep the faith." Like we're in some conspiracy together.

Waiting for my own proctor to arrive, I skim the information sheet about commissary privileges I got along with my clothes. More rules, more ways to get things wrong. But I don't need to worry about them since my parents had made it very clear that I wouldn't have any spending money here. Then, whoa! I have to look twice before fully comprehending that there's a hundred dollars in my account. But how?

Then it hits me: Kyle's mom.

What can I do, what can I do, she kept asking me before I left.

"You can leave me alone," I said. "Please just leave me alone."

But no. Marianna has to put a hundred dollars into my commissary account. Did it even occur to her that nobody in this place would ever get that much money? That if people found out I had that much it would only make my life worse than it already was?

Well, fuck her. She can't make me spend it.

Nonetheless, I can't help reading the list of items you can buy, things I'd really love to have, things that would make my day-to-day life so much easier to bear:

Personal tablet

Music and video games

Earbuds

Hand cream

Soda

Snacks

Microwaveable meals

Bottled water

God. How I'd love a Pop Tart or a bag of Skittles. A bottle of clear, cool water without the gross, metallic taste of the tap water here sounds like heaven. But all I buy is deodorant, shampoo, and a pocket calendar, to mark off the days.

Not one single thing I don't absolutely need.

Never Forget

Back at Cottage Five, Officer Hadley hands me a letter with Marianna's beautiful handwriting on the rich cream envelope, its return address embossed in gold. I have to close my eyes and take deep breaths to keep from tearing it up on the spot. Instead, I slip it into the pocket of my khakis.

"Grace! You got a letter!" Jessica says, materializing beside me. "I'm so glad you got one and, guess what? I got one, too. Look—" She pulls a wallet-sized picture from the pocket of her khakis. "Damien."

He's sitting in a miniature fire truck, a fireman's hat perched on his head, grinning—an ugly, round-headed child, who looks a lot like the fat, broad-faced monsters in *Where the Wild Things Are*.

"Oh, my gosh. He is so cute," I lie.

Jessica beams. "I *know*." And rattles on about how her mom and grandma will be bringing him to visit soon and she *so* can't wait to see him.

Marianna's letter feels heavy in my pocket. I want to read it and get it over with, but it's impossible to get away from Jessica until lockdown is called at eight. Finally, we line up, file down the corridor to our rooms, close the doors behind us. When everyone is in, Officer Hadley locks the doors with one loud click, like a gunshot. Pathetic that it's such a relief to be here. Goddamn cement walls. Goddamn hard bunk. Goddamn plastic crates.

Goddamn red eye, blinking. I'm tempted to make a face at it, or worse—something Electra told me she'd done herself. "Worse" being dancing naked in the eye of it.

"It's like playing Roulette," she said. "You never know which room the custody officer is spying on, so you might totally get away with it—or not. And I got away with it."

"*That* time," I said. "What's the matter with you, anyway?"

Electra just laughed. "Pretty much everything," she said.

I should fix her up with Kyle, I think. Maybe he'd fall madly in love with her, and the two of them could live happily ever after, creating mayhem. Something I no longer have any interest in myself. I'd erase that ridiculous chaos tattoo Kyle talked me into getting, if I could.

I sit down on my bunk and open the letter.

Dear Grace—

I know that you and Kyle can't write to each other, so I'm writing to you to let you know that he is doing okay at school. Of course, he misses you terribly. When I call, you're all he talks about. I miss you, too—both of you.

I hope you know how sorry I am that your punishment was so harsh and how much I hate to think of you in that place. I've put some money in your commissary account for whatever you might need. If there's anything else that I can do for you— anything at all—it would make me happy to help. Meanwhile, please write to me and let me know you're okay so that I can reassure Kyle. We are both worried sick about you.

Take good care of yourself, Grace—and know how much you are loved.

Hugs,

Marianna

Hippy Prep, that's what Kyle called the school his parents talked the judge into letting him attend instead of going to jail. The brochure advertised confidence-building activities like hiking and rock climbing. Yoga and meditation to encourage reflection, forgiveness, and self-love. Individual and group therapy, of course.

"There's even Equine Therapy," Kyle said. "Since when do horses have personal issues?"

He was trying to cheer me up, I knew. Make me laugh.

We were on the phone because we weren't allowed to see each other. We weren't supposed to be talking to each other, either—but my parents still didn't know about my iPhone, so they wouldn't find out.

"Grace?"

"Yeah," I said. "I'm here."

"We just have to suck it up and get this shit over with, right? Then we can be together for real. That *is* going to happen."

"Yeah. I know." I didn't say what I was working myself up to tell him: I can't afford to love you anymore. I just can't.

I reread Marianna's letter, then tear it up into tiny pieces so I won't be tempted to read it again—and do my best to put both of them out of my mind.

The First Time

Kyle's a year older than me, but we were in the same grade. His parents kept him in preschool an extra year so when he played sports, he'd be a year older and stronger than the other kids in his class. It turned out he didn't like sports, though, which was okay with his parents because They Only Wanted Him to Be Happy. He also didn't like the expensive private high school where they sent him. When he purposely failed all of his classes as a first semester sophomore, he said he'd done it because he wanted to be with real people, and his mom was so proud of him for being a real person himself that she built him his own apartment over the garage. He thought Jeeps were badass, so that's what he got as a reward for promising to work hard at the new high school (which he didn't). And Ray-Ban aviator sunglasses so he'd look cool driving it.

They had boatloads of money. His dad was an architect who designed environmentally efficient buildings all over the world and was always traveling. His mom was a painter, who, Kyle told me, had inherited millions. She spent nearly every waking hour in her studio when she wasn't off to New York or LA for some art show. They had a live-in housekeeper, Mary, who'd been with them since Kyle was born and considered him one of her grandchildren, calling him Sweet Boy.

I couldn't even imagine a world where everyone adored me. For a long time, I couldn't believe that Kyle had chosen me. *Why?* I was average-looking; you'd never pick me out in a crowd. My body was okay, but nothing special. I was smart, but school-smart, and Kyle didn't care about that. I wasn't funny, like he was.

But there he was. Every morning he pulled up in the Jeep to take me to school. He walked me to my classes, sat with me at lunch. He was waiting at my locker when the last bell rang, and we'd go get our espressos and talk. Then we'd go to his apartment and make out and talk some more. If it wasn't too late, he'd play Doom or Rocket League for a while and I'd read until it was time for him to take me home.

I'd never had a boyfriend, just dumb crushes—the kind where, if the boy acted like he might like me, too, I was so mortified I couldn't say a word. But being with Kyle was easy, like having a best friend only better because of the whole different kind of closeness. Once, during a sex-education lecture, before we hooked up, our Your Health and Well-Being teacher said, "There is only one first time. Make sure your first time happens in a way that, later, you won't wish you could forget."

At the time, it made me want to put my head on my desk and cry because my first time had been with Jack. I thought I'd never want anyone to touch me again. That even with someone I loved and who loved me, I'd see Jack's face in my mind's eye, hear the ugly sounds he made, feel that searing pain inside me. But Kyle was so gentle with me. It was as if he knew I'd been wounded somehow, knew it would take time for me to be ready for the next thing.

Then one day, we pulled into the driveway and his mom was just getting out of her van.

"Shit." His hands tightened on the steering wheel and for just a second I thought he was going to back out of the driveway and go—where? But he turned off the ignition and we got out.

"Sweetie," his mom said, beaming. Then, "This must be Grace! I'm Marianna. *Call* me Marianna." She was tall with long blond hair caught up in a messy bun. She wore a huge, white, men's shirt over her jeans.

I held out my hand, but Kyle's mom threw her arms around me and said, "Let me look at you—" and she did, for what felt like forever.

"Smile," she said. "If Kyle loves you, we do, too."

I couldn't help smiling.

"Help me carry this stuff up to the studio?" she asked, sliding the van door open.

Kyle went rigid beside me but didn't protest. The three of us carried rolls of canvas and tubes of paint and cans of turpentine up the three flights to the attic where she worked, a huge space, light falling in from the skylights above, the white walls hung with her paintings—big, abstract, bursting with color. One corner of the studio was like a small, cozy living room, with a couch upholstered with fading roses and matching easy chairs. There was a coffee table cluttered with art books, and I thought it would be a wonderful thing to sink into the couch and leaf through them.

But when Marianna invited us to stay for a cup of tea, Kyle said no, we couldn't, we had homework to do, which was a total lie because we never did homework together. Kyle didn't do homework at all.

I didn't say, "Your mom seems nice," when we left the studio. I didn't say, "Why do you hate her?" Neither of us said anything at all until we got to his apartment and he put his arms around me and whispered, "I want you, Grace. I love you so much. Please. Now."

He took me by the hand, stood me in front of the full-length mirror on his closet door and it was as if he was giving me a lesson in myself—starting with my hair, twisting a curl around his finger, moving it down between my eyes, to my nose, then tracing the outline of my lips, the arc of my chin into my neck.

I stood absolutely still, my whole body a tuning fork.

He unbuttoned my shirt, undid my bra. I shrugged them away. His finger kept moving, just that one finger, like a paintbrush, and I watched myself in the mirror, watched him touching me until my eyes started to glaze over and my knees went weak and he picked me up like I was a baby and carried me to his bed.

"You believe I love you, don't you," he asked, when we were through. "That I'll always love you? Always."

I did believe him, which should have made me happy. Instead, I started to cry.

"Grace," Kyle said. "Shit. Did I hurt you?"

"No," I sobbed. "No."

"What then?"

I shook my head; I couldn't speak—and he drew me closer.

"Tell me," he whispered.

But how could I tell him I was crying because the feel of his gentle, reverent hands learning my body had been so lovely, so different from Jack's ugly hands pawing me, his foul breath making me gag.

"Grace. Tell me," he whispered again.

"It's nothing," I said. "I can't help it. I just love you so much. I love how I feel so safe with you."

Because I knew the deeper truth would break his heart.

Back to School

I know how to do school. I loved school when I was a little girl, I felt happy there. There were rules for right and wrong, and if you followed them, you would be rewarded by the teacher's approval. There would sometimes even be prizes—for reading the most books, for being the first one to learn your multiplication tables, for writing the best story with that week's spelling words. Your work might be posted on the Good Work Wall. Every single classroom of my childhood had seemed like a home to me, safe and full of wonders.

Teachers loved me because I worked so hard, I was curious, I was eager to learn. They felt sorry for me, too, because they knew something was wrong, it had to be, because my parents were so disengaged at parent conferences. But they never asked me if there were problems at home.

Then in sixth grade there were different teachers for every subject, different rooms, different kids in every class. It seemed like the bell was always ringing, I was always gathering up my stuff, lugging my heavy backpack through the crowded halls where kids shouted and jostled and bumped into me, sometimes by accident, sometimes on purpose.

The on-purpose part started when I came back to school after the awful time at church camp: Zoe started being mean to me, too. She was popular now, why wouldn't the other kids follow her example? She was pretty, blue eyed with blond hair that fell in waves down her back. She had cool clothes. She was funny. I woke up with an anxious stomach every school day wondering what she'd do or say to make me feel bad. There were new kids who might have become friends, but there was no way I was going to risk letting anyone get too close.

I wake up with that same familiar stomachache on my first day of the Wabash Valley Promise Academy, with Zoe on my mind. Not that I'd heard a word from her since that awful camp, let alone when I got in trouble. Still, I wonder if Zoe feels bad about what happened to me, if she cares.

Like I should be worrying about Zoe when I need to concentrate on how to get through the day. Be careful, I tell myself. I can't afford to be uncooperative, but I also can't afford to be seen as a suck up. I need to fly under the radar. The rules in the Wabash Valley Handbook are simple, all about respect and control.

Students who do not follow the rules and/or create any kind of disruption will be sent to in-school suspension and will receive a conduct report.

Teaching staff should be respected like custody staff.

Students must go directly from class to class without stopping, walking silently down the right side of the hall, with their hands behind their backs.

Students must not exit a classroom without a pass from the teacher. If found outside a classroom in a non-passing period without a pass, they will receive a Conduct Report.

Blah, blah, blah.

It's the unspoken rules that scare me, the ones the girls make themselves—and you don't know what they are until you break one and, suddenly, there's threat and tension everywhere. Who the couch in the day room belongs to, who gets first choice of the board games, who can make fun of one person or another and who can't.

We line up when it's time to go, Jessica behind me whispering that she really, really hopes we're in the same classes, and me thinking, *please, please, please, no.* We march out into the morning, girls from all of the cottages crossing the yard like little parades, merging near the school. Just my luck: Electra ends up right in front of me. And I think *please, please, please, no* about Electra, too. It was a fucking miracle she hadn't gotten both of us in trouble during orientation.

"New girls, step forward," the custody officer waiting in the doorway says.

Electra turns and grins at me. "Long time, no see."

"No talking," the custody officer says—and gestures for us to follow.

"Bitch," Electra mutters behind her back.

The principal, Mr. Overbeck, is a stern man with a haircut that makes the top of his head look like a landing field. Big, like a football player. "Welcome to the Promise Academy," he says, "where attitude is everything. You will thrive here if you understand this. If you don't—"

He splays his hands. "It's all up to you, ladies. So, do your best to get off on the right foot. Now. Let's get to your class assignments."

The good news: I'm not in Jessica's class.

The bad news: I'm in Electra's.

It's the smart class, Mr. Overbeck tells us over his shoulder, as he escorts us to the classroom. "An honor we expect you to make yourselves worthy of."

"An honor *of which* we expect you to make yourselves worthy," Electra whispers.

Exactly what I was thinking.

The other girls look up momentarily when we enter the classroom. There's maybe a dozen of them. Ha, I think. It's probably the size of Kyle's "small, intimate" classes at Hippie Prep. There might even be some of the same idiotic motivational posters there. But there would also be computers and all kinds of AV equipment, nice furniture, bulletin boards teachers had labored over, and mountain light pouring in through the windows—as opposed to battered desks, skittering fluorescent lights, a long view of the loopy concertina wire on top of the high fence through the bank of windows, and mostly empty bookshelves.

The teacher, Ms. Bowman, directs us to two empty seats toward the back of the room. Surprise! No lecture about attitude. She just explains that this is Humanities class, which includes English and Social Studies. Mainly, the class is filling in workbook pages because everyone is on a different level. Also, people come and go, and you can't always be getting some new person up to speed.

Electra rolls her eyes. "And this is the *smart* class."

Ms. Bowman hands each of us a new grammar workbook. "Write your name in the front," she says. "Then start at the beginning. If you get to something you don't understand, raise your hand and I'll call you to my desk."

I leaf through the pages. Nouns, verbs, adjectives, lay/lie, their/there/they're, commas, periods, colons, semi-colons—stuff I learned in grade school.

It turns out, all of my classes are easy, with workbooks you go through at your own pace—going backwards sometimes to correct mistakes you made the day before. And thank God, Electra calms down after a few days, only occasionally rolling her eyes or making a sarcastic comment under her breath. The only thing that makes me anxious is Humanities reading group, which can get Electra agitated if she's in one of her moods. Every few days we get a dog-eared copy of a story, always the same kind of Dead White Guy story English teachers in real school make you read—some copies so old that the edges of the paper feel like silk. We have to read the story at least three times, take notes, and be prepared to discuss the questions at the end of the ninety-minute period.

"Could we please just once read something relevant to *us?*" Electra bursts out the day Ms. Bowman hands out a Hemingway story. "And maybe not by a man?"

Ms. Bowman sighs "I wish," she says. "They don't give us much to work with here."

Electra looks at her, gives a little shrug, then bends over *Indian Camp.*

It's a story about a kid whose dad, a doctor, takes him across a lake to a camp where he's been called to deliver a Native American woman's baby. He brings no anesthetic, so some of the men have to hold the her down. The boy watches. The woman's husband is in the top bunk, with a wounded foot—and when the baby is born and the doctor stands to tell him all is well, he discovers the man cut his throat with a razor.

Some of the girls start arguing about what the kid saw and what freaked him out the most. *"Obviously,"* one says, "he saw his dad cut into the woman and saw him take the baby out, which was so gross he probably didn't *really* see anything after that."

"No way," another one says. "He saw."

"Just the guy's head tipped back, that's all."

"Well, duh, how disgusting would that be? At least seeing a baby being born is *natural.*"

"That guy who killed himself?" a third one says. "He didn't even see the baby get born. He slit his throat because he couldn't stand to hear his wife screaming. Fucking pussy," she adds.

"Jesus," Electra says. "Who cares about *that*? Doesn't anybody wonder about why the kid's father took him there in the first place? I mean, seriously. What kind of person would purposely let a kid see something no kid should ever see, something he knew the kid would never, ever forget? He should burn in hell for that. And what about that poor baby, born into such a world of violence and grief?"

The whole class is stunned into silence by such passion. But that doesn't stop her.

"You know what I'd like to see?" she goes on. "I'd like to see that story from the pregnant woman's point of view. How do you think she felt with that little kid and his uncle looking on like she was some kind of— curiosity. It would be a whole other story, that's for sure."

"You could write that story," Ms. Bowman says.

"An *Indigenous* woman should write it," Electra says. "That's my *point*. Like anyone would read the story if a brown woman wrote it, though. Or any woman. It sucks how men even get to be in charge of stories."

She looks at me, raises her fist, and I bump it—before remembering it's not a good idea to take sides with anybody in this place.

Gibbous Moon

I wrote "Gibbous Moon" in fat black marker on poster-board, the letters getting smaller and more cramped as they reached the edge. And beneath it, *Gibbous is one of the fazes of the moon. It is almost round, but not round because the other part is hiding. Sometimes the gibbous moon gets bigger in the sky the next day. Sometimes it gets smaller. Bigger is waxing. Smaller is waning.*

Also on the poster-board was a chart with little drawings of the moon on it. Each night, before bed, I looked at the moon through the window in my bedroom at my mom's house and at my dad's, too, and drew the way it looked. Fat and yellow the first night, then getting smaller and smaller, till it was like a fingernail clipping, then nothing at all, then getting bigger and rounder until it was a whole fat circle again.

It was my fifth-grade science project. Everyone in my class had to do one and now they were propped on our desks for Parents Night, each of us standing by, ready to answer questions the parents asked.

I could still feel my fingers gripping the pencil in my hand, my tongue between my teeth, trying to get each moon just right—and later writing the report. Jack used to help me with projects but then he stopped. I was a big girl now, he said, and didn't need his help. But, really, he was just tired of me.

It wasn't fair. The other kids' parents helped them, and their projects looked way better than mine. The only reason I didn't cry was because Ms. Orr, my favorite teacher ever, said I did a very good job. So did Zoe's parents, who had given me a ride there because my mom was running late at the office. Some other parents said it, too, but only because they felt sorry for me, and I didn't look up so they wouldn't ask me to explain anything.

My dad didn't come. It wasn't his night. My mom didn't get there until almost the end. When she looked at my moon poster, she said, "There is a misspelled word here, Grace. It's supposed to be P-H-A-S-E-S not F-A-Z-E-S. Honestly, you're in the fifth grade! Is there a reason you didn't bother to look your words up in the dictionary to make sure they were spelled right? You should be ashamed of yourself."

I was always ashamed of myself. I was ashamed that I didn't know how to be the daughter my mom wanted, that Marlys hated me and there must be some reason for it, that sometimes I was jealous of Briony even though I loved her more than anyone else in the world. I was also ashamed that I'd grown breasts and some hair in my girl place because it made Jack sad. He said he wished I could be a beautiful little girl forever.

Then I got my period, which was gross, and he didn't touch me anymore. I was glad about that; sometimes when he touched me it hurt and made me cry. But it made me lonely, too, because I missed how Jack always hugged me after he did it and said I was his girl. Now I touched myself sometimes, which also made me feel ashamed.

I could feel myself about to cry just thinking about it, but I closed my eyes tight to keep the tears from coming because Ms. Orr was watching us with a worried look and if she came over and said something nice about me to my mom it would only make her get madder.

Group Therapy

Ms. Miller welcomes me to Cottage Five group therapy, which I have to attend every week now that I've completed orientation. "Everything we do here is meant to help you adjust," she says. "So, the more of yourself you give, the more likely you are to adjust and the more likely you'll be able to do your time here successfully. That is what we all should be striving to accomplish."

We? Kyle's voice whispers.

Ms. Miller looks about twelve. Her cheap black suit, the pink blouse, the scuffed black pumps make her look like she's playing dress-up in her mother's clothes. She sits up straight, clipboard on her lap, and smiles hopefully at the girls of Cottage Five, gathered around her in a circle of plastic chairs in the dayroom. We're in various states from torpor to agitation—yawning, nodding off, rocking, twitching, tapping feet, picking at open sores.

Except Wren, on the couch, head bent over Harry Potter, as usual.

And Jessica, who raises her hand when Ms. Miller asks if anyone would like to share.

Someone snickers.

But Jessica ignores this. "Remember, last time you said it would be good for us to write a letter to someone we were mad at, but we didn't have to send it? That it would be, like—helpful, just to write down how we feel? Well, I wrote one to my dad."

"Would you like to share?" Ms. Miller asks her.

"OK, sure," she says, and takes a folded-up piece of notebook paper from the pocket of her khakis.

Dear Daddy—

I guess you don't know where I am and probably you don't even care, because why would you, the way you went and moved in with that lady you work with and hurt Mama so bad we had to move away. I didn't want to go. Even if she was right and you didn't ever come back home like she said I didn't want to leave my friends and have to go to a new school. I liked the one I went to just fine. For your information, the only people in my new school who were nice to me at all turned out to be bad people who got in trouble all the time and pretty soon I was getting in trouble too. That's how I ended up in this place, which is jail. I did very bad things that I am sorry for. Also, for your information I have a little boy now. He's almost two years old. His name is Damien. I know it was wrong to have sex before I got married, it was a sin, but I am not sorry I had Damien because I love him more than anything in the whole world and because of him I opened my heart to the Lord Jesus Christ. When I get out of this place, I will never leave him like you did me. I hope you are sorry.

Your daughter,

Jessica Lynn Whitman

Oh, God. I slump into the silence that follows, embarrassed for Jessica, scared to think she doesn't understand how dangerous it is to put herself out there like that. Also pissed at myself because I feel responsible for protecting her.

Even more pissed that Ms. Miller looks directly at me and says, "Girls, what would you all like to say to Jessica about what she read?"

But before I can think of something to say that won't make Jessica feel even more attached to me, Destiny leans forward so she's almost in Jessica's face. "He fuck you, your dad? He got two or three buddies who like to fuck you, too?"

"No!" Jessica says. "He never did that!"

"Then, girl, what is your big problem?"

"Destiny!" Miss Miller says. "Language! Let me remind all of you, we don't use that kind of language here. And we respect one another's paths and their pain."

"Okay, *intercourse,*" Destiny mutters. "Whatever."

"Enough!" Ms. Miller jots something on her clipboard. "That's a point off for today, Destiny. You need to calm down. If you want to participate you need to do it in a positive way."

Destiny heaves back into her chair with an exaggerated sigh.

"Why do people have to be so mean?" Jessica asks me when it's over.

"Just ignore them," I say. "Who gives a fuck what they think?"

"*Grace.* Don't say that word. We can't."

"Fuck, fuck, fuck," I say. "So, turn me in."

"No!" She blinks back tears. "I'd never do that, Grace. You're my *friend*. I don't want you to get in trouble."

"Look," I say. "Don't worry about me, okay? And don't expect me to worry about you, either."

"Okay," Jessica says, in a small voice. Wounded.

FIVE

Kind of Like Boo Radley

Before I met Kyle, I gobbled up books like they were candy. Jack read to me when I was little, the same books over and over—*Don't Let the Pigeon Drive the Bus, Green Eggs and Ham, Guess How Much I Love You.* He bought me a scaled-down reading chair, with its own little ottoman and a cozy throw draped over the arm in case I got chilly.

When Jack Camp was over, I discovered the library not far from my mom's house and rode my bike there most days. I loved the afternoon bustle of children and their mothers, the long, narrow corridors of books opening into quiet spaces with tables where you could do your homework, chairs where you could curl up and read for hours. I checked out some books again and again: Harry Potter, *A Series of Unfortunate Events, The Mysterious Benedict Society.* Of course, *The Hunger Games.*

But the book I loved most, the one I checked out more than any other, was *To Kill a Mockingbird.* The book made me both happy and sad. Happy because, reading it, I was Scout and Atticus Finch was my father. Sad because when the book ended, Atticus disappeared from my life—just like my real dad did. And here's another sad thing: I found a battered copy on the bookshelf in the day room and started rereading it but I wish I'd just left it sitting there because the N-word keeps jumping out at me, making me feel cringy. It feels wrong even to let that ugly word into my mind at all and keeps me from loving the story like I used to.

Kind of like *Harry Potter* being spoiled for me when I found out how J.K. Rowling felt about trans people.

When I mention this to Electra, she agrees. "It sucks about J.K. Rowling," she says. "Although, the books tell the truth about how things are. What are we supposed to think about *that?* And in *To Kill A Mockingbird* Atticus Finch proved that Black guy didn't rape that woman and that stupid town convicted him anyway, which I guess was a big deal when the book was written. Also, it was cool how Scout ended up being friends with Boo Radley."

This makes me think of trying to explain the book to Briony, who couldn't see past the grand opportunity for a game.

"Let's Play Boo Radley!" she said. "Okay. You be Boo and live in my playhouse and I'll be Scout and live in the gazebo. Pretend I'm not allowed to try to see you. Pretend my mom is Calpurnia and Daddy is Atticus and they say, 'Leave Boo Radley alone, he is a troubled man.'"

"You're smiling," Electra says.

And, despite the fact that I'd made up my mind not to tell anyone here about Briony, I tell her the story.

"Ted, her dog, was supposed to be Bob Ewell because he could roll over dead. And no problem that it was just the two of us. Briony said it was okay we didn't have Jem and Dill." I imitated my sister's bossy voice. "'We do *not* need boys.'"

"Word!" Electra says.

I get all the way to where Briony insists we go inside and steal boxes of raisins from the pantry for Boo Radley to find, when Ms. Bowen says, "Girls, do your reading now."

I bend to my book but can't concentrate because I keep thinking about how much I miss my sister. Which inevitably leads to missing Kyle—not only, well, his *body,* but how he was always saying things I'd never thought about before.

Like, your parents are assholes. Why do you even want people like that to love you?

Like, where has trying to be perfect for them gotten you?

Or, wouldn't it be nice to feel good for a change?

Yes, I thought. It really, really would. So, I did everything Kyle said would make me feel good and most of it did, though some only made me forget.

Drugs were stupid. And it wasn't like I didn't know that. Breaking into people's houses, stealing stuff was even worse. The thing is, I was so wrecked I just didn't care. I still don't, not really, except for the fact that because of it Marlys and my dad said I couldn't see Briony anymore.

But I know Briony still loves me because right before I got arrested, I sneaked into the backyard of my dad's house, put a note for her in an empty flowerpot, and left it in exactly the same place she'd left Boo Radley's presents: *Hey Briony, I miss you. Are you okay? Love, Grace.*

For a few days there was nothing, then Briony answered: *Dear Grace, I'm really mad my mom and dad won't let me see you because YOU ARE MY SISTER and it's wrong to not let sisters see each other. I hate them. I don't care what they say, you are the BEST SISTER EVER. I miss you and love you. If you want to run away, I will. I mean it. Just leave me a note and I will be ready. Love, Your Whole Sister Briony.*

After I read the note, I crept out into the alley, sat down by the fence, and cried so hard I made myself throw up. There was snot all over my face, my hair was wet with tears, I hiccupped until I could barely breathe. Finally, I calmed down and wrote back: *Dear Briony, YOU are the best sister, I love you forever. Never, ever forget that. But don't hate your parents, they only want you to be safe, they can't help it. They don't know I'd never ever hurt you, even though they should. I wish we could run away together but it wouldn't be right. We can write notes,*

though, and leave them in this secret place. Kind of like Boo Radley, kind of like spies.
Love, Your Whole Sister Grace.

Wren in the Day Room

Wren always sits in the exact same place in the dayroom: the farthest corner of the couch in the farthest corner of the room. She's always reading Harry Potter. She's the one person in Cottage Five I have any interest in talking to and those first few days I tried to talk to her about the books. Wren was never rude. She just looked up with a sad expression, and I realized it was because I was making her come up out of the story. It was where she lived, how she survived.

"You want to stay away from her," Jessica said. "I told you. She stabbed that pastor thirty-seven times—with a *kitchen knife*. And not only that! She got into a fight with Lauvette one time before you came and you think she's this tiny, quiet little thing, but she is sooo not. I don't know what Lauvette said to her, but she was talking and all of a sudden Wren flew off the couch—really, that's what it seemed like—and Lauvette was on the floor screaming and crying. There was blood everywhere, they had to pull Wren off her—and she was still fighting when they dragged her away. I'm just saying—"

But I'm not afraid of Wren. It doesn't bother me one bit that Wren killed the pastor. I imagine her plunging the knife into the soft places on his body again and again, watching the blood spurting, pouring, pooling. The knife handle sticky with it by the time she was through. I'd like to talk to her about what that felt like. But even if there were someplace private and no one else could hear, why would I want to make Wren sadder and more lost than she already is? So, I just sit quietly beside her.

I can breathe sitting next to Wren, close my eyes for a few moments, let the noise of the dayroom settle in around me—and it begins to feel as if we're carrying on a kind of conversation without words. I'm grateful for Wren's silent acceptance, the zone of quiet around her, not to mention the brief vacation from Jessica, who sits at a table on the other side of the room, doing her homework or watching TV, glancing at me from time to time with a hurt expression. I feel sorry for Jessica; I do. I sit awhile with her most evenings, too—listen to her talk on and on about Damien. I help her with homework; sometimes we play a board game. The later it gets, the easier it is to be with her. The sleep meds kick in, her voice slows until, finally, it stops all together. All sound in the dayroom stops, except the television blaring whatever show the bickering girls settled on and, beneath it, the ancient heating system kicking on and off, like rattling breath.

Jessica Is Writing the Story of Her Life

No surprise. Jessica raises her hand when Ms. Miller asks who wants to earn cooperation points by writing about their lives.

"You get a free notebook if you do it." Ms. Miller takes a pink composition book off the pile in front of her and hands it to Jessica. "Writing can be a very healing process, you know. You'll surprise yourself sometimes, write something you didn't know you knew."

"Wait," Bree says. "If you write it, you already knew it, yeah?"

"Good, Bree. You're absolutely right. But there are things we only know subconsciously and sometimes writing makes them float up."

Bree rolls her eyes.

I'm tempted by the notebook, but shake my head when Ms. Miller looks at me hopefully. It's hard enough here knowing what you know without adding things in your subconscious that want to stay hidden. Not to mention what if that something that *floats up* you don't want anyone to know and then somebody reads it. There's no privacy in this place.

"Listen," I say to Jessica. "You might want to be careful what you write."

"Why?" she asks. "I want to write the story of my life for Damien. The whole truth of it. So, he won't make the same mistakes I did and, no matter what happens, he'll know how much I love him and how the Lord Jesus

Christ gave him to me to help me get my life back on track. How He put me in this place to make that happen.

"If he hadn't, I'd probably be dead. And I'll tell you something else. I believe He sent *you* here so we could be friends and take care of each other. I truly do."

"Jessica. I don't believe in Jesus," I say. "I've told you that."

"You think you don't," she says. "I understand. I thought that, too—and then He was here, waiting for me. Just like he's here for you right now, Grace. I pray every day you'll find him. He's always here for all of us, watching, even if we don't know it."

Really, I want to say. So, he was up there at the Right Hand of God, both of them watching Jack do what he did to me, waiting for—*what?* I'd like to share Kyle's view of Jesus with Jessica. Because if she's worrying about my immortal soul, whoa! It would totally blow her mind to hear what Kyle has to say on the topic.

He laughs inside my head. "If there is a god," he says, "maybe he did match you up with that girl—as punishment for not believing in him. Did you ever think about that?"

The Gospel According to Kyle

"If Jesus came back tomorrow, like they're always threatening he's going to do, the shit would totally hit the fan," Kyle said. "All those people and their rapture? Going the *other* way. He'd go for Wall Street first, you know, like how he and his bros busted into that temple and took out all the assholes ripping off people who had to change their money and the people selling animals for slaughter and shit, not to mention the priests who were getting a cut of everything. Then those mega churches with their slick preachers talking people out of their money so they can have their mansions and Mercedes.

"Dude, he'd be so triggered if he saw all the Christian crap you can buy—as opposed to giving your money to the poor, which people would do instead of spending it on stupid shit if they actually paid any attention to what he was saying. Light The Night with Jesus glow sticks. Christian bling pens, Christian drumsticks, Christian dishtowels. Five-hundred-dollar Bibles," he -said. "Morons. Do they not know the cheap ones say exactly the same thing?"

What got him started was, he Googled "Amazing Grace tee-shirts" because he thought it would be cool to get one for me and landed on a Christian website. They had "Amazing Grace" tee shirts, all right, but not just plain "Amazing Grace" tee-shirts. They all had crosses or pictures of Jesus or glittery sunrises. One had "Saved With Amazing Grace," he told me—one word to a line, with the first letter of each word in a different color. They spelled SWAG going down.

"Can you believe that?" he said. "SWAG."

He had to have the tee-shirt he gave me custom-made. No way was he going to give that site a fucking penny.

He recited a list of ridiculous tee shirts you could buy. How did he remember them all?

"I've Got Glitter in My Veins and Jesus in My Heart."

"My Lifeguard Walks on Water."

"Cool Christian Chick."

"Ask Me to Pray For You."

"Property of Team Jesus."

There was an orange shirt exactly the same color of a Reese's wrapper with "Jesus, Sweet Savior" on it—and "King of Kings" inside the shape of the peanut butter cup.

"Reese's should sue them," Kyle said. "They really should."

I never quite knew how to deal with it when he got on a rant. Part of me loved how he got so indignant about things that were hypocritical or unfair; I was touched by how sometimes he was as pure and earnest as a child.

But part of me wanted to say, "Look around! How do you persist in being so surprised?"

And when I actually did say that to him once—it was the only time he ever got mad at me.

"What's the matter with you?" he said. "That shit should always surprise you. When it stops surprising you, when it stops making you pissed out of your mind, you might as well be one of them. You might as well be dead."

He was right, of course. I thought of Marlys's gold cross, inlaid with diamonds, her bracelet made of tiny gold crosses linked together and its matching earrings. Her "Make a Joyful Noise" tote bag. The doormat that said, "God Lives in This House."

Also, there was the Jesus fish license plate on her car—which Kyle replaced with the Darwin fish that had legs on it and Marlys didn't even notice until a month or so later when someone at church mentioned it.

Witnessing, Marlys called this display of her belief. Everything you did to draw attention to your faith was a testament to your commitment to Jesus.

"The real Jesus would make her go batshit," Kyle said. "He'd be grubby and long-haired, like a hippie, schlepping around in Birkenstocks, preaching peace and love. Plus, talk about surprise: not blond and blue-eyed, not even white. She'd probably think he was a terrorist, being from the Middle East and a radical and all."

"Did you ever believe in Him?" I asked. "Like, when you were little?"

"I didn't even know about Jesus when I was little," Kyle said. "Santa Claus, the Easter Bunny—I had no idea there was more to Christmas and Easter than that. Then in middle school I had this friend, Justin, who was Christian, but weird Christian—like, his family belonged to this house church in kind of a bad neighborhood. It wasn't like real church at all: no pastor. People—women, even kids—took turns giving sermons and doing other religious stuff, rituals, whatever—which Justin's dad told me was the way it really was when it started. Christianity, I mean. He said there's this whole other part of the Bible with whole different gospels that got cut out when they started having priests and popes and all that on account of those gospels were about peace and love instead of scaring people to death about going to hell. I looked into it, and what he said was pretty much true."

He laughed. "My parents were totally wigged out. They wouldn't admit it, though. You know my mom: I could be an axe murderer and she'd say, 'Kyle is so gifted with the axe.' Anyway. I messed with their heads about it for a while. But there was no way I was actually going there. I mean, I believe Jesus lived. I believe He was a righteous dude. The coming back from the dead thing? Give me a *break*.

"I'll tell you one thing, though: If I did believe I wouldn't do it half-assed with fish license plates and shit like that. I'd be a monk, one of those guys who holes up in a monastery and prays and contemplates and only comes out to beg money for the poor. Otherwise, what would be the point?"

Electra's Flight

It's Halloween, a crisp autumn day—blue sky without a single cloud. Only a few yellow leaves are left on the trees in the woods beyond the high fence that runs along the river. I didn't even know there was a river so close— you couldn't see it before the trees started losing their leaves. But there it is, silver and sparkling in the sun.

What are those trees whose leaves turn bright yellow, the last ones to give in to winter every single year? I wonder and then think of Jack, who always knew such things, who took me on nature walks in the neighborhood and sometimes to the woods nearby, where he would pull me down to his lap and we'd sit, leaves drifting down, birds chattering, and he'd name the trees around us and the birds, which he knew by their songs. I remember nothing of what he taught me during these nature lessons—*clearly*. Just the other thing he sometimes did when he took me to the woods, and I am *not* going there this afternoon. I'm going to enjoy being outside, the warm sun on my face, feeling a surprising camaraderie with the girls in Cottage Five.

It's a tradition, Officer Hadley told us. Every Halloween, the yard crew blows the fallen leaves into huge piles and the girls bag them. The cottage that bags the most leaves wins a pizza party—real, order-out pizza, not the gross, gummy pizza they make here.

"We. *Are*. Winning," Lauvette says. "We are working our—" She glances to make sure Officer Snap isn't listening and she's not, she's talking on her radio. "—fucking asses off," she concludes in a low hiss. "All of us. We are the ones eating that pizza tonight."

She looks so fierce I can't help laughing.

Lauvette gives me a look, then starts laughing, too.

We're an army of workers, ten cottages of fifteen or so girls each, wearing green sweatshirts and khaki pants and work boots, fanned out across the grounds. We work in teams of two, one girl shoveling into the huge piles of leaves with her hands, scooping as many as she can hold, the other holding the big garbage bag open to receive them. No slacking, no half-filled bags. Officer Snap and a half-dozen other custody officers are there to make sure of that.

Of course, I'm stuck with Jessica, who's slow and wheezing and can't stop talking about how she wishes she could play in the leaves with Damien, like she did with her dad when she was little. How it was so much fun when he still lived with them, before he went off to live with his girlfriend who had so many kids he didn't have time to be her father anymore. She's so mad at him, she says, but she still loves him, though she wishes she didn't.

"Stop flapping your mouths," Officer Snap says. "Use that energy for something useful."

"I hate her," Jessica whispers when she's out of earshot. "Why is she so mean?"

"Because she can be," I say. "There's nobody to stop her."

"Well, that's wrong."

"Ha. Name one thing that's right here," I say—immediately regretting my words because I know exactly how Jessica will respond:

"You are," she says. "You're nice to me. You're the best person I know."

Officer Snap looms. "Lowery, Whitman," she says. "What is it you two don't understand about stop flapping your mouths?" She takes the little black notebook from her shirt pocket. "Two demerits," she says, marking them down with obvious satisfaction.

"Sorry," Jessica whispers when she's gone. "I always—"

"Shhh," I say.

I don't give a damn about the demerits, they were worth it because, in the enforced silence that falls between us, scooping, pivoting, opening my arms to let the leaves fall into the open bag feels like dancing. I work quickly, efficiently, taking the bag from Jessica when it's full, shaking it to balance the leaves inside, then setting it down. The bags will be closed later by the grounds staff because we're aren't allowed to have the twists, which we might somehow turn into who knows what kind of weapon.

Scoop, pivot, drop, scoop, pivot, drop, scoop, pivot, drop.

Lauvette and Kenyae work independently, like dervishes. Maria and Bree work together like a machine. Kaylie and Destiny touch hands for a long moment each time Destiny bends to dump a pile of leaves in their bag—giggling when Lauvette gives them the evil eye. Only Wren has no partner. Dreamily, she lets leaves drift from her hands into a bag propped beside her, most of them missing it. Officer Snap doesn't say a word to her.

I look up and see Electra across the yard, standing with her hands on her hips, looking up, her orange hair dazzling in the bright sunlight. How does she get away with it, not doing a thing while the other girls from her cottage are at work all around her? And what is she looking at? I glance up. Nothing but sky.

Suddenly, she whoops and runs toward a huge, untouched pile, launching herself into it, creating an explosion of leaves, then rolling around like a toddler until the guard from her cottage gets to her, grabs her arm, and marches her away—Electra laughing wildly. Or is she screaming?

Do it, Kyle's voice says in my head. *Come on. Do it.*

God. How fabulous it would feel to drop the leaves I'm holding, take off like Electra did, and fly into our pile. But I turn back to scooping, all the while wondering whether I should be glad I knew better than to do something that foolish myself or whether seizing the chance to fly, even for a moment, would have been worth it—whatever the cost.

SIX

What Is a Day?

I numbered my pocket calendar backwards so I could count off the days until my release date, May 31. The number of days had freaked me out so bad when I added them up that I almost threw the calendar away. But no way am I just going to float through the days. I mark off each one, filling in the whole square with my pen until it looks like a black hole, a reminder of how stupid I was to end up here in the first place and the small victory of having survived it so far. I keep the calendar in my room, where nobody can see it but myself, and marking is the last thing I do before lights out. If I could, I'd wait to mark it out until my very last thought before sleep.

All that time to think inexorably leaves me wondering, what is a day, anyway? How can one zip by, and another creep along so that it feels like an eternity? How can a day be over, but still be alive inside you, *more* alive than the day you're living now? Every single night, after lights out, days I've lived all through my life come and go in my mind's eye, vivid and complete, until they begin to float into each other and reconfigure into dreams. Sometimes I wake up in terror; worse, sometimes I wake up unbearably happy until the dream dissolves and I'm back in my locked, windowless room, the concrete walls closing around me.

Then there's the question of the future, which seems like a high cliff I'm walking toward, the imagined drop, the free-fall all the more terrifying for its inevitability. And. Each day survived brings me closer to the moment I'll have to face my parents, who won't want me any more than they did before I got in trouble. And what if Marlys still won't let me see Briony?

I mark off the first day of November, which I thought would be satisfying. A new month! Progress! But the whole page of blank squares makes me feel half-sick. It also makes me wonder how many of those days Electra will be in solitary. That must be where she is. She wasn't in school today; she wasn't with the other girls from her cottage at dinner.

I've heard terrible things about solitary. The cells like closets, the beds without mattresses or blankets, the food—even worse than the food in the cafeteria. It's so dark you can't tell night from day. And rats, though maybe Amber and Maria were just trying to scare me with the rats.

But even without rats, Electra is bound to freak out, confined like that, and do something to keep her there even longer. She's so stubborn, she might never get out. I was so determined not to be drawn in by her, not to get attached to anyone. But I've been worrying about Electra since the guards took her away yesterday. I keep hearing her screaming. Cottage Five won the pizza party, but I was so upset I couldn't finish my two pieces and they were thrown away, which pissed off the other girls. Like it was my fault I wasn't allowed give what I didn't eat to one of them.

Right now, it seems like I'm going to be locked up in this place forever. Maybe Officer Hadley had been right when she said it was a bad idea to mark off the days. "Better to live them," she said. "Let them make their own rhythm."

But how can I *not* be thinking constantly about all these lost days of my life, doing whatever I can do to feel like I have some control over them?

I wonder if Electra is counting, too

Theme for English B

Kyle once said, "Watch out when English teachers give you some vague-ass assignment and tell you to be creative. Because you turn it in and they give it back to you, bloody from their red pens. You can't grade something creative," he said. "It's wrong. They should stick to grammar and shit. And, you know, Shakespeare—whoever. Besides if they were creative, they wouldn't be English teachers. They'd be poets."

All I knew was that if you wanted to be creative you were better off to keep it a secret. I used to write stories. It didn't exactly make me happy to write them; it was that, when I was writing, I forgot where I was, I forgot all the things that made me sad. I didn't even realize that the stories themselves were sad until I showed one to my middle-school English teacher, who said, "This is very good writing, Grace, but it's so dark. I don't think it's a good idea for young people to dwell on sadness."

Yeah, the stories were about terrible things happening and kids managing the best they could. They had happy endings, though. Eventually a kind person would come along and sweep them into the life they were meant to have. The teacher watched me closely for a while after that, which worried me. The stories weren't about me. I wasn't that dumb. I'd *never* have written about Jack. I was worried, though. If the teacher called my parents to tell them she was concerned about me, my mom would be furious and my dad would be scared to death that Marlys would find out and make a big deal about it.

I wrote stories after that, but not as often, and I always erased them from the computer once I downloaded them to a flash drive that I hid in the toe of an old pair of UGGS knock-offs in my closet. I stopped when I met Kyle because, for a while, he made the miserable parts of my life feel so much smaller. But what happened to that drive, I wonder. Is it still there, or did my mom have one of those cleaning sprees she has sometimes when she's in a bad mood and toss the boots into a Goodwill bag? Not that it matters.

Though its mortifying to think some girl trying on the boots, finding the flash drive, pulling the stories up on her computer and laughing her head off because they're so bad. I feel sorry for them, my poor stories. Sorry I even wrote them because if you can't tell the truth in a story, why bother to tell it at all?

And I'm sure as hell not going to tell the truth here. So, I can hardly keep from groaning when Ms. Bowman, says, "I thought it was time to introduce a little creativity in our lives. Each of you is going to write a poem."

Electra, back from her three days in solitary, does groan.

"Now, now," Ms. Bowman says. "You girls think you can't write a poem, but I know you can. And I'll help you. So will Langston Hughes."

"Who?" Someone asks.

"Langston Hughes," she repeats.

"He's a brother," Dierdre, says. "But it ain't February."

Ms. Bowman regards her quizzically.

"Black History Month," Deirdre says. "February."

"You can read Black poets in November," Electra says. "Jesus. There's no rule."

"Electra," Ms. Bowman says.

Electra raises her hands, as if in supplication.

Ms. Bowman ignores her, launching into a lecture about Langston Hughes and how his poetry spoke to the issues of his people and his time. How it challenged and raised questions. "So," she concludes. "I've chosen a favorite poem of mine to work with: 'Theme for English B.' And what we're going to do is: I'll read it several times—a poem needs to be heard more than once to be really heard—and then I'll hand you your own copy that you can use as a model to write a poem of your own."

"What do you mean, model?" someone asks.

"I mean, that you think of the poem kind of like a box or a certain size and shape, then put your own words and ideas into it. You can use similar line lengths and rhythms. Even some of the words, if you want to."

"That's cheating," Deirdre says. "You get in trouble in real school if you copy."

"Not copy," Ms. Bowman says. "*Model.* You use the structure of Langston Hughes's poem like a room to put your own words into. That's all. It's an exercise. Not like a poem you'd publish and pretend you'd thought of it on your own."

Deirdre looks skeptical.

Ms. Bowman looks like she wishes she could just drop the whole thing and tell us to open our workbooks. But she soldiers on. She reads "Theme for English B" twice, slowly, with feeling, wrings out a few sullen observations about what the poet meant to say, then hands out the copies, clearly relieved to leave us to work on the assignment until class is over.

But almost nobody is working. They're sitting, slumping, staring, twitching, daydreaming, nodding off to sleep. They probably figure they've frustrated Ms. Bowman enough so that she won't make us hand in our poems. Or maybe, like me, their minds are blank. Electra's scribbling madly, though, chewing the tip of her pencil for a moment, then bending again to the words that keep coming until the bell rings. Then she folds her paper, slips it to me with a grin when she's sure Ms. Bowman isn't looking.

"Read it later," she whispers. "Alone."

And I do, in my room, just before I mark off the day in my calendar.

Electra's Theme for English B

'Instructor says,

Go home and write
A page tonight.

Let that page come out of you—
Then, it will be true.'

Here's the truth—
I'm seventeen,
think white trash, born in Muncie, Indiana.
Left a shit school there for one in Peru—
not the country Peru
—a dumpy Hoosier town

Here I am—
prison near the river that runs
beyond the high fence,
barbed-wire spiked-sky
Paths crisscrossing dead grass,
each one, dead end
think, just like my life

But, okay, I go up the steps of the Promise Academy,
stay in line, stay to the right, enter classroom—
think, filled with losers
—sit down, write this truth

What's true?

I can say I'm what I feel,
what I see,
hear—
Wabash Valley Juvenile Correctional Facility,
I hear you:
hear you, hear me—we too—you, me,
talk on this page.

Think
white trash,
think basketball and hot dogs,
yellow mustard squirting from the bun

Think
running in heat until you puke.
Think
loud, headbanger music

Here's truth—
I think white trash means different
because, yeah, I like to read,
but what *I* like to read—
not what some bitch teacher tells me.

And, here's the truth—
once in some social worker's car,
I liked this music with no words,
crazy notes going every which way

So maybe I'm the same abyss as everyone else

Will my page be
as empty
as I am?

Being me,
nothing
like what you wanted

Do you wonder what I've learned from you?
I will be a part of you and you of me.
That's American!

But, truth—
what did you learn from me?

Instructor all old and middle class

and a whole hell of a lot more free
So, here's my truth for English B.

Whoa. I read it again. And again. And again.

Who is this girl and why did she write this?

And why did she give it to *me?*

A Willing Vessel for His Grace

Dr. Welty is one square on the boardgame of my life here at the Wabash Valley Juvenile Correctional Facility for Girls. *Move the game piece forward,* I tell myself before every visit. But every time I take my seat before Dr. Welty, I start crying. I still can't bring myself to speak. It's her voice, — so much like Belle's—, what else could it be?. But I didn't even have a real relationship with Belle. She was just my only safety. Belle cleaned Jack's house every Tuesday, she was kind to me, she hugged me like she must have hugged the grandchildren she always talked about, she baked cookies for me every single Tuesday: peanut butter, my favorite kind. They were warm from the oven, the smell of them still in the air when I came in after school.

I think about Belle every time I'm here but, today, rage rockets me, shocking the hell out of me, and my tears stop. I can't possibly be angry at Belle. Why in the world would I be angry at Belle, who never failed to treat me kindly, who always made me feel safe?

Then left.

I think of Zoe's mom, who I also loved, who also made me feel safe—until the day I overheard her talking about me on the telephone.

"Grace," Dr. Welty says.

When I don't answer, she sits patiently, her hands—she has beautiful hands, I notice, perfectly shaped fingernails polished the color of seashells—folded on her desk.

"My office is a safe place," she finally says. "Nothing will hurt you here. I promise. You can spend your time with me just feeling safe, just sitting quietly for an hour a week, if that's what you want to do. I understand why you would want to do that."

I clench my jaw. Five minutes pass, ten. I have to make my whole body go rigid to stop from fidgeting in the chair, or scratching the itch on my nose, which moves to my forehead, to my ear. I try the counting trick to calm myself, but since I'm determined not to move my head, all there is to see is Dr. Welty herself. So, I stop counting, close my eyes.

But it's as if Dr. Welty hit the remote to turn on the movie in my mind—and I am sitting before that creep Christian counselor my dad and Marlys made me go to because of my "bad choices." Missy, with her gummy fake smile, the trendy black glasses she probably wore to make her look smart, and so much make-up you could make a trench with your fingernail if you ran it down her cheek.

"I've been where you've been," Missy said at our first session.

"And where would that be," I asked.

Missy unbuttoned the cuff of her silk blouse, raised it so I could see scars from cutting on her arm. "I've felt without hope, without purpose, without love so I know—"

"You know fuck-all about me," I said.

"I know God loves you," Missy said.

"Like I believe in God," I said. "Why would I?"

Missy smiled that looney Christian smile. "But He believes in *you*," she said, "and He is with you always. He's with us right now, in this room, I swear it. He's here for you, Grace, and I'm here as a willing vessel for His grace to work in your life."

"Willing vessel?" Kyle said when I told him. "Are you shitting me?"

"For His grace," I said. "Don't forget that part. 'A willing vessel for His grace.'"

"Fuck her," he said. "You don't need their grace. You don't need some fucking counselor to tell you who to be."

"Grace," Dr. Welty says.

Here. Now.

"I don't need this," I say. "I don't need you. I don't need anybody. I just need—"

"To get out of here," Dr. Welty says. "I know that. I understand it. And you will get out. Very few girls are here more than six months or so and, so far, there's no reason to believe you'll be here any longer than that yourself. So, you can just wait it out. Like I said earlier, you can come here every week and just sit and feel safe for an hour."

She gazes at me, hands folded on her desk.

Why doesn't she say the next thing: "But—"

Duh. Because she's not an idiot, because she knows I'm not an idiot. I'm already running the buts through my mind and she doesn't need to lay them out for me.

But you'll probably be here longer if you're not responsive in therapy, and I have no choice but to report it if you're unresponsive.

But you'll be wasting your time here, wasting the opportunity to get your shit together.

Well. She wouldn't say "get your shit together."

I can't help smiling at the thought.

Dr. Welty raises an eyebrow.

But I'm not going there.

"Quiet it is then," Dr. Welty says. "Maybe quiet is what you need right now."

And suddenly I feel calmness settle upon me in this blessed quiet she allows.

Zoe's Mom

I loved my best friend Zoe, but I *adored* her mom. She had red curly hair and green eyes and she was always smiling and called everybody Sweetie or Honey. I loved Zoe's dad, too. He used to be a football player and got a kick out of picking up Zoe and me, one under each arm, and carrying us like footballs, laughing when we yelled at him to stop because he knew we didn't really want him to. I loved her sisters Hannah and Hope, who were in high school, and sometimes on Saturdays would give us makeovers if we begged really hard. Monica made Zoe a friendship bracelet, but she didn't make one for me.

When I asked Zoe, "We're best friends, why do we need Monica," Zoe said, "It's not good to have only one friend, my mom told me." This hurt my heart so much because, once, I heard her mom tell someone, "Grace is here so much it's like we have an extra daughter," and I thought it meant she wished I was her daughter the way I wished she was my mom. Which I thought kind of made Zoe my sister.

Then one day Zoe and Monica sent me downstairs to ask Zoe's mom for treats, but I stopped just before I got to the kitchen. "The thing about Grace," Zoe's mom said to someone on the phone, "she's a sweet girl, but she's so *needy*—and, I don't know, there's just something off about her. I can't quite put my finger on it. Those dreadful parents, of course, especially her mom. *She's* a cold fish if there ever was one. And the dad, you've got to love those guys who screw up with one family and think they can just start over with a new one. Not to mention the stepmom, what's her name, Marlene, Marla, whatever. Let me tell you, she's a real piece of work.

"I feel sorry for Grace," she went on. "I do, but she's way too attached to Zoe. She gets sulky and quiet when Zoe invites other girls to play with them. And she's so intense, she's always, I don't know, watching, listening. Like she's trying to memorize us. It's a little creepy. She called me 'Mom' the other day and didn't even realize it. I thought, whoa, I have my fair share of kids already, the last thing I need is another one—and a needy, messed up one to boot."

I crept back through the living room, up the stairs to Zoe's room.

"Where are the treats?" Monica asked, in a mean voice.

"I didn't get any," I said. "I don't feel good. I have to go."

I waited for Zoe to tell me to stay, but when she saw me lingering, she just said, "Okay, see you tomorrow."

Jack's house was only a few blocks away and I set out toward it. My mom didn't like me to go home when no one was there, even though I had a key. It was before I changed, when I knew Jack would be glad to see me.

Diagramming Sentences

Jessica is bent over her English worksheet, erasing what she's written so many times that she makes a hole in the paper. "I can't do this right," she wails to Officer Hadley, who comes over to see what's wrong. "I don't know how and now I've torn the worksheet and Ms. Grimble will take away my neatness points and I *need* those points."

"Oh, no. Not my neatness points," Kaylie whines.

Officer Hadley shoots her a look, then turns and asks me to help— like I'm Jessica's friend and of course I'll want to help her. It isn't the first time. Officer Hadley is no slouch. She knows I just don't have the guts to treat Jessica the way the other girls do. So, I reach for Jessica's worksheet, slide it over so both of us can see it.

"Thank you, Grace," Jessica whispers.

"Sure. No problem," I say.

"Diagram These Sentences," it says on the worksheet. The sentences are simple, not like the ones I had to diagram in my English class in real school.

"You start with nouns and verbs," I say. "You learned about parts of speech in grade school, right?"

"I don't know," Jessica says. "I guess. But if I did, I can't remember them. I never can remember stuff like that. I pray on it. But I just can't."

"You can," I say. "But praying won't make it happen. You have to study. Didn't you do that in school before you came here?"

No response.

"It's okay," I say. "I'll help you. It's not really that hard: A noun is a person, place, or thing. Verbs are action words, like walk or run. Barf is a verb," I add, to make her smile.

She doesn't. She has this blank look in her eyes.

And all of a sudden, I realize why she struggles so hard: she's stupid. And then I feel a wash of grief for her and guilt at that word being my first thought. Not stupid. We use that word—stupid—all the time for people who do and say things they didn't think out and for ignorant people who choose not to see what's right in front of their eyes. For people who don't agree with us, for people we don't like, and that isn't what I mean. What I mean is that her brain is not going to let her learn this. That there's a whole lot of stuff, especially school stuff, that some people may never be able to learn, no matter how hard they try.

"Listen," I say. "Let's not worry about memorizing a bunch of stuff right now. Diagramming is really just about figuring out which words go with each other." I tear a page from her own writing pad and write the first sentence on Jessica's worksheet.

The big dog howled at the full moon.

"Okay. Where's the first person, place or thing?"

"'Dog?'" Jessica asks.

"Right. That's good! See, you do know nouns. Now, what action did the dog do?"

Jessica thought a moment. "Howled?"

"Yes," I say. "So that's the verb.

I draw a horizontal line on a fresh piece of paper, write "dog" on the left side. Then I make one in the middle and write "howled" on the right side of it.

"Which of the other words go with dog?"

Jessica looks slightly hopeful. "'The'? ' Big?'"

"You got this!" I raise my palm for a high five and Jessica slaps it, giggling.

Then I make two slanting lines beneath "dog" put the words on them. "Which words go with howled?"

Jessica points to "moon", and I make a straight line next to "howled", put "moon" on it.

"What about 'at' 'and' 'the' and 'full'?"

"Um. Under 'moon'?"

"Right. See, it's not hard when you break it down? You did it. I just drew the lines."

"Only because you helped," Jessica said. "It's easy for you."

"Which is because someone helped *me*. I had this great teacher who taught us how to know where words go in a diagram. She said, 'Think of a sentence like it's a house and every word is a room in it. The most important words get to live on the top floor.

I put a check mark above *dog, howled, moon.*

"'The others live downstairs. See? Without 'dog', 'the' and 'big' aren't necessary. Without 'moon', 'the' and 'full'—same thing."

"Oh," Jessica says. "Cool. That makes sense."

"Okay. So, let's try another one."

We work through the sentences on the worksheet, Jessica brightening as we go.

When we finish, she writes "I Love Damien" on her writing pad, then diagrams it. "Every word is on the top floor," she says.

"Yes," I say—and blink back tears.

I wonder what Ms. Orr would think if she knew I was teaching her lesson in *prison*, if she'd seen anything in the eager, needy little girl I'd been that made her think I might get myself in trouble someday. I hope she doesn't know what I did, but teachers seem to have some kind of radar about the kids they've taught so, probably, she does. It was in the paper, after all— humiliating my family, possibly even making my mom lose clients. I still get that shriveling feeling inside when I think of it.

So, I think about Ms. Orr instead, how I loved diagramming sentences in her class. It made me happy to think of a sentence as a house of words; once I made Ms. Orr laugh when she said that the way some words beneath the line were pocketed into others made her think they lived in closets.

"I like the way you think, Grace," Ms. Orr said—and I smiled the whole rest of the day.

If I could just go back to Ms. Orr's classroom where I always felt safe and—loved? *Did* Ms. Orr love me? It had felt like she did. She loved all of her students, of course. She said that often. But I had believed she had a special feeling for me. When I discovered *The Hunger Games*, she told me she'd read it, too, and sometimes at recess we'd walk around the playground together and talk about our favorite characters. She showed me other books in the library I might like: *Divergent, Esperanza Rising*. The Percy Jackson series, based on mythology, which I loved.

And Ms. Orr wasn't afraid of sad books, like some teachers were. The whole class read *The Bridge to Terabithia*, which made some of us cry, but Ms. Orr said it was okay to cry because the story was so true and real. We read *Nightjohn*, too, the story of a slave girl, Sarny, who secretly learns to read. Ms. Orr played the part of the audio book where the slave who teaches her gets caught and Mr. Waller, the plantation owner, orders the overseer to chop off his toes. Some kids' parents got mad about that. It was too much, they said. Their kids were upset. But we just went right on talking about the book in her class.

"Why didn't the plantation owners want their slaves to learn how to read," Ms. Orr asked us. "Think about it. What were they afraid of? What was the worst thing they could imagine?"

The question gave me a cold prickling on the top of my head. "They were afraid—" I said, then stopped because I hadn't raised my hand.

"Go on." Ms. Orr said.

"They were afraid of them being smart," I said. "They were afraid if the slaves learned how to read they could figure out how to get away."

"Bingo," Ms. Orr said. "Very good, Grace. You are absolutely right. Bad people who are put in charge of things are always afraid of losing their power. They like it when we're dumb, when we're not curious, when we don't dig deep to try to understand what's happening in the world, when we just go along because it's the easiest way.

"Never forget this," she said. "Smart, thinking people scare them to death."

Is that Officer Snap's problem? I wonder. Is that why she seems to single me out—and Electra, too—because she knows we're smarter than she is, that we see what some of the others don't see, and terrorizing us is the only way she knows to keep us in her power?

I diagram a sentence on a horizontal line in my mind's eye: "Officer Snap fears me."

Then I add words, slanting and pocketing them until the house Officer Snap lives in is so chaotic she'll never find her way out of it. *The odious pig-eyed asshole Officer Snap fears me greatly because she is stupid and I am not and she knows I will get out of this fucking hellhole but she will be here forever because the only thing in the whole world she is capable of doing is making unfortunate girls' lives even more miserable than they already are.*

Then, in spite of myself, I feel sorry for her because I see another thing about stupid, the weaponized ignorance kind of stupid: it can make you mean, the weapon. Not that this is an excuse for how Officer Snap treats us, just—well, it makes me sad.

Hoops

Captain Donnelly has girl crushes, and Electra is one of them, which is creepy. She'd make her a proctor, for sure, but Electra doesn't qualify because she gets in too much trouble. She's already been back to solitary, I don't know for what this time, but it was another three days. She pretty much always has a yellow bracelet, sometimes red. So, Captain Donnelly just watches her on the basketball court, her whistle held loosely in one hand. Though, I have to admit I like to watch Electra, too.

She dribbles like she's dancing, shoes skidding on the wood floor. Sweat rains from her orange hair, her body wet and shining. She paws the free throw line like a colt, then swoosh. No net. Every single time.

Nobody stands still in the Shape Up Zone, so I watch while I walk, moving my head sideways, straight ahead, sideways, straight ahead as I go so I don't miss anything. Like how Captain Donnelly gives the tiniest nod, a physical *yes*, when the ball goes through the net.

The bell ending our session ends and Captain Donnelly hands Electra a towel when she comes off the court.

"You could totally make her your slave," I say, in the locker room.

Electra raises her hands, cups them as if holding a basketball, then flicks her fingers open to let it go. "I like the irony," she says. "Hoops being *my* factor of control for a change, when always before it was hoops trying to control me."

"Meaning what?" I ask. "There couldn't have been a whole lot of girls in your high school better than you are."

"Meaning you had to pay, like a couple of hundred dollars. The coach wanted me, she said she could find someone to pay my fee, but I said, fuck that. Then they'd think they owned me. Plus, what about all those other girls who want to but can't afford it?"

"You have to pay to play basketball? *School* basketball?"

"Yeah. In most places." She gives me this look. "Little rich girl," she says. "Probably not where you live."

"I'm not rich," I say. "Why does everybody here think that?"

"Straight teeth." Electra opens her mouth, revealing her own crooked ones.

"That's crazy."

She shrugs. "Look around. You'll notice now. Anyway, don't worry. It's not your fault."

"I'm not rich," I say again.

"Okay. Describe where you lived before you came here. I'll decide."

I think of my mom's townhouse condo, the walk-in closet, the Jacuzzi in her bathroom. My dad and Marlys's big brick house on one of the nicest streets in town. I guess I am rich, at least compared to Electra, though it's not as if either of my parents give me any more money than I absolutely need.

"Well?" Electra says.

I shake my head. There's no point trying to explain to Electra how lonely I feel in my parents' beautiful homes, how it hurts to know that neither of them wants me with them. They'll take care of me, obviously—my mom, because if she dropped the ball, my dad and Marlys would make her life a living hell. And Dad, he'd probably feel too guilty if he totally abandoned me.

.

"Okay. Forget it," Electra says. "I was being an asshole. Really. We're all fucked. It doesn't matter where we came from. I'm sorry. Okay? Grace?"

"Okay," I say.

"Good," Electra says. "Back to hoops. Number two irony: hoops got me in here. That's where they found me, the fucking police: shooting hoops on the playground of this elementary school. Middle of the night.

"I was so out of that hellhole my social worker put me in. I had everything I needed in my backpack, some money I stole from my foster mother's purse—which, honestly, I was owed, considering they spent jack shit of the state-money on me. Enough to get a bus ticket to somewhere.

"Anyway. I'm walking downtown—a long way, but I could've made it—and I see a basketball on the playground of this school. A decent one, too. Probably got left outside after recess. And there's basketball hoop, too. So, I figure what can a few shots hurt? Pretty soon, I'm having the time of my life, trash talking to nobody, I literally can't miss. Until a cop car pulls right up onto the playground.

"I take off running, leave my stuff behind. But do I get one of those fat cops, who can't run a block? Nope. I get a fucking track star. A *woman*. She's got me down, getting ready to put on the cuffs, and I'm yelling my head off. I'm like, 'I didn't *do* anything. What did I do?'

"'Curfew,' she says.

"I'm like, '*What the hell?* Curfew? Come on. I'm eighteen, look at my ID.'

"She was a total badass. She was, like, 'You don't want me to look at your ID, baby. 'Cause I'm willing to bet that would make just one more charge when you're in plenty of trouble right now. Curfew. Resisting arrest. And we got a call about a foster kid missing. Underage girl with red hair and the bad habit of running away. Name of Electra. You know anything about her?'

"Shit," Electra says. "I was busted. No way I was going back, though, so I jerked away from the cuffs, which got her off balance, and took off again. Obviously, she caught me.

"Long story short: Here I am. And here is where I'm going to stay," she adds. "Until I'm eighteen and foster care can't touch me."

"You *want* to stay here?" I ask.

"Damn straight. Three meals a day, a bed with nobody in it but me. Why do you think I'm always getting in trouble? I've got a short sentence. Runaway. But every time I fuck up it gets longer. I've done the math. I know how often I have to fuck up to stay here, I know when I can stop—on my eighteenth birthday. Then I wait it out and I'm gone."

"You're kidding, right?"

"I am dead serious," Electra says. "Officer Donnelly can fuck me all she wants in her mean little mind, but she can't touch me. Dogface Snap can push me around, but she doesn't dare *really* hurt me. Solitary. Honestly? I don't mind the quiet. I mean, five foster homes, living on the street in between, doing whatever I had to do to stay alive. I'm tired of that shit."

She laughs. "Plus, it's like getting a college degree in 'crazy' here. I'm taking notes, you know, for my future in psychology. So, yeah. I'm as serious as a heart attack. Anybody wants to find me? 'Til the day I'm eighteen. This is where I'll be."

What I'm Thankful For

Every Thanksgiving, right after the prayer, Marlys made everybody at the table say something we were thankful for. All the leaves of the dining room table had been added, stretching it to the full length of the big room. Marlys held court at one end, my dad on the other. Marlys' mother was there, a dour wrinkly woman I took some pleasure in seeing only because I could tell Marlys was going to look just like her when she got older—along with a collection of guests from church Marlys referred to as lovely people with nowhere to go. It was possible, I thought, that Marlys invited them because every year they said what they were thankful for was Marlys herself and her good work. Which maybe took the edge off for her when, every year, Briony said, "I'm thankful for Grace."

It makes me smile to think of this now, sitting in group on the day before Thanksgiving. Ms. Miller looks at me hopefully, having just made the same request.

"I know the holidays are painful for you girls," she says. "But there's always something to be thankful for, no matter how small. Let's each say something we're thankful for today."

No way am I going to say I'm thankful for Briony, like I've done every Thanksgiving since Briony was born. Nobody in Cottage Five even knows I have a sister and I'm not about to divulge that piece of information now. Briony is my secret, my joy. And anyway, "thankful" comes nowhere near expressing how I felt yesterday when my name was called and Officer Hadley handed me a letter from my sister. My heart had sped up just at the sight of her still child-like writing. There was no return address in the upper right corner, I noticed even before I opened it. Smart girl. If the letter had been rejected for some reason, it wouldn't be returned for Marlys to find.

Dear Grace—

They said you were in a special boarding school and nobody was allowed to write to you there, but they are liars. I snooped and found some papers in Daddy's desk, so I found out where you really are and I am really, really mad.

NUMBER 1. Because they lied, which they shouldn't have. Aren't they always saying WE shouldn't lie?

NUMBER 2. Because it isn't fair. You are the best person of all and I don't care what you did you shouldn't have to be in a place that is really a prison.

I know because I googled it. That's how I found the address. So I can write to you whenever I want. But you can't write back because, you know. Not like I care what they think. Just, if they find out, they'll get mad at you instead of me. Like they always do. Cuz that's how they are. Which is also unfair and also makes me MORE mad at them.

Anyhow. School is stupid, so there's nothing to write about that. Halloween was stupid too because you weren't there. I still hate piano lessons. So, I guess that's all for now. DO NOT WRITE BACK. I will keep writing to you, though. I promise. I stole a whole card of stamps from that place where my mom keeps them in the kitchen. She was, like, I know I had more stamps than this. Ha. Ha.

LOVE from your whole sister and your loyal friend, Briony

"Grace?" Ms. Miller asks now, and I can hear the *please* in her voice. "Why don't you start? Tell us something you're thankful for."

I take in the circle of girls, slumped in their chairs, looking less defiant than usual. Maybe Ms. Miller is right about them feeling bad about missing the holiday.

"No school tomorrow?" I offer.

"Yes!" Ms. Miller beams. "Or Friday!"

"Yeah, no school," Lauvette agrees and in a rare moment of solidarity, and "No school" makes its way around the circle like dominoes falling.

Jessica's last. "No school *and* Damien," Jessica says. "But mostly I'm thankful for Damien."

"Of course," Ms. Miller says. "Of course, you are. You'll miss him tomorrow, I know," making a perfect transition to the topic of the day: Coping with Sadness During the Holidays.

It's okay to acknowledge our feelings, it's normal to be sad when we can't be with our loved ones on the holiday. We should take advantage of our recreation time—exercise lifts the spirits. We should pray for comfort and guidance. Remember happier times.

Does Ms. Miller think this catalog of clichés is news to *anybody?* Does she actually believe that remembering happier times is going to make us feel better instead of worse? Right now, for example, I'm remembering last Thanksgiving. Not the afternoon meal at Marlys and my dad's house, but dinner with Kyle and his parents that evening. Not turkey and all that other crap that makes you feel fat and sleepy, but steak—at a really nice restaurant downtown, waiters in starched white shirts and black aprons, light jazz playing low. I was anxious about going. I liked Kyle's mom, but he was always so tense around her; I'd be meeting Kyle's dad for the first time. What would we talk about? What if I said something wrong? What should I wear?

Then I found the most amazing dress laid out on Kyle's bed the Wednesday before Thanksgiving: the exact chocolate brown of my eyes, fitted at the waist, flaring to mid-length, tiny silver buttons from the V of the neck to the hem.

There was a note from his mom.

"I just couldn't resist buying this. I think it looks exactly like you."

"Oh, my God. Kyle. This must've cost a fortune," I said. "I can't—"

"Yes, you can," he said.

And I wanted it so much, it was so beautiful. But what in the world did Kyle's mom see in me that had made her think I belonged in such a dress?

Kyle picked it up. "Try it on," he said.

I shrugged off my hoodie, pulled my t-shirt over my head, stepped out of my jeans and Kyle handed me the dress, which he had unbuttoned to the waist. It fit as if it had been tailor-made for me. The top followed the contours of my breasts without being too snug, the narrow sleeves came exactly to my wrists—and the way the rich fabric of the skirt fell in folds around my calves made me think of twirling in a party dress when I was very little.

"You look awesome," Kyle said.

I *felt* awesome. It seemed to me that, wearing that dress, I could go anywhere and believe I belonged. It made me feel loved because I knew this was why Kyle's mom had bought it for me.

On Thanksgiving night, when the waiter brought the drinks we ordered, Marianna (she had told me to call her Marianna, though I still felt too embarrassed to do it) lifted her glass. "Grace, we are so thankful to have you in our lives," she said. "We are so, so glad Kyle found you."

"Hear! Hear!" Kyle's dad said. "To Grace."

He and Kyle lifted their glasses, touched Marianna's with a clink.

All of them smiling at me.

And I'm supposed to feel *better* remembering this?

Bullshit. It makes me feel like dying.

SEVEN

A Visitor

When my name is called on visiting day, I think maybe my dad feels guilty and has decided to come even though he said he wouldn't. But it can't be him because it's Saturday; he and Marlys always volunteer in the soup kitchen at their church on Saturday. It's probably best if I don't see him anyway. Just the sight of him might make me tell the real story of how I ended up here, which really started when he left all those years ago. What good would that do? He has a whole other life with Marlys and Briony now, and Marlys doesn't want me to be a part of it. Right now, I'm not. For all I know, that's a relief to my dad, even though he probably feels bad about it.

Or maybe he doesn't. I don't know.

Still, it would be the most amazing thing to walk into the visiting room and see him stand and smile and open his arms when he saw me. I'd walk into them and bury my head in his chest like I used to do when I was little, breathe in the scent of soap and shaving cream.

But Kyle's mom is the one waiting. She looks like an exotic flower in her embroidered peasant blouse, her dangly silver earrings, her round black reading glasses on a chain around her neck.

My knees go wobbly. I can't help being drawn to the energy radiating from Marianna, but at the same time just looking at her makes me feel like I can't possibly bear one more second in these hideous clothes, the awful sneakers worn by who knows how many other caged girls, my unwashed hair pulled back in a ponytail.

"It's easier when you don't have visitors," Destiny said one Saturday, when the girls who had them had been called from Cottage Five to the visiting room. "They make you remember how shit it is here. You see it in their eyes."

"You're just jealous," Amber said.

Maybe she was, I thought. But it was also true that Amber came back from visits with her mom and sister and sat on the couch in the day room for a long time, eyes closed, head bent, and wouldn't talk to anyone.

The room itself is depressing, dotted with tables, each with some variety of a family sitting with their inmate—all women and children, not a father among them, and boyfriends aren't allowed. There's a clock covered with steel mesh, like all the others here. Dull green walls, speckled linoleum floor grimy at the edges. High windows frame rectangles of gray sky. It smells overwhelmingly of sweaty bodies and Lysol and the food the girls' visitors are allowed to buy for them from the vending machines and heat up in the microwave—burgers, pizza, beef stew. There's the beep and clunk of those machines, the rise and fall of conversation, children laughing and bickering as they play with the pitiful collection of toys kept on a low shelf—a yellow plastic dump truck, dolls with ruined hair, some books, a beat-up Fisher Price barn. A teetering stack of extra orange chairs in one corner reminds me of those tall, striped Dr. Seuss hats that certain druggy guys find so amusing.

Jessica waves wildly, grinning, holding a fat, fussy Damien up so I can see him.

I raise my hand, grateful for the moment to get my bearings, get myself under control before walking to the table where Marianna sits alone.

The visiting rules, posted on the wall, allow one hug at the beginning of a visit and one at the end. Of course, Marianna jumps up to hug me. I let her, but stay stiff in her arms, unnerved by the mix of lavender and paint that takes me back to being in her studio on those afternoons with Kyle.

"Oh, dear God," she murmurs, her voice breaking. "I'm so sorry you're here, I'm so, so sorry—you know I tried—"

I know. She tried to convince my parents to send me to a school for troubled girls; she even offered to pay for it, insulting my parents, who icily refused.

"Tell me," Marianna says, when we sit down.

"Tell you what?"

"How you are, why you haven't written. We went to see Kyle for Thanksgiving and, Grace, he's a mess. He's so worried about you. I promised him I'd come. Sweetie, why didn't you answer my letter?"

"Because I was afraid I'd get in trouble if they figured out you were Kyle's mom. I'm not supposed to have anything to do with him at all, you know. But you don't need to worry. I'm fine. You didn't need to come."

"I did. I needed to see you." Marianna presses her eyes with her knuckles. "For Kyle—and myself, too. I needed to be sure you're—Oh, my god, how can they have put you here? It's worse than I thought it would be—a *prison*."

Which annoys me. She thought it would be what? Just one step down from where Kyle is? Mediocre food? No equine therapy, no spa?

"Grace," she says. "Please. Tell me. Has anyone hurt you?"

Well. There's the bruise on my arm that never goes away because Officer Snap always grabs me in exactly the same place, the nasty shove on the basketball court that made me bite down on the inside of my mouth and draw blood, sneaky jabs from Maria and her family. It would only freak out

Marianna to know. It's not a big deal, anyway. I'm used to it. The thing is, as much as I hate it here, nobody can hurt me in any way that matters. Not like my parents hurt me with their indifference, not like Jack who hurts and keeps hurting me in my dreams. Not like Kyle, who made me love him. How could I possibly explain this to Marianna? Besides, she'd be so mad she'd report it to the warden and my life would get worse than it is now.

"Grace! Hey, Grace!"

Jessica, Damien squirming in her arms. I can't help smiling at the flicker of alarm in Marianna's eyes.

"I'm so excited you have a visitor," Jessica says. "I just knew you'd get to meet Damien, I told you, I prayed on it—and here you are. Look Damie." She turns so Damien is facing me. "It's Mama Jessica's best friend, Grace."

"Me down," Damien says.

Jessica holds him tighter. "So, are you Grace's mom?" she asks Marianna brightly. "I'm so glad to meet you. I'm so glad you came for her."

"I'm her boyfriend's mom," Marianna says. "And who is this beautiful boy?"

Jessica puffs up like a pigeon. "My son. Damien. He's almost two."

"Goodness," says Marianna. "Look at his darling little suit."

He's wearing a shrunk-down version of a man's suit, complete with little striped tie. It's all askew from struggling to climb out of Jessica's arms.

"Damien," she says, sharply.

"Mama," he whines, looking over her shoulder at the woman who is obviously Jessica's mother. She's rail-thin, her face looks caved in, she has meth mouth, like Jessica—so bad it's obvious from across the room.

"*I'm* your mama," Jessica says. "Mama Jessica. You know that, honey. Say 'Mama Jessica.' Come on, now, say it."

"Want *Mama*," he says. "Down." And takes off like a shot the moment she lets him go.

"He's so little," Jessica says miserably. "He gets confused."

"I'm sure he knows," I say. "And he's really cute. I'm glad I got to meet him."

"Okay," Jessica sighs. "Well. I guess I should go back."

"How old is that girl?" Marianna asks when she's gone.

"Fifteen."

"Dear God," she says. "And those teeth—"

"Meth. That's what she's here for, drugs. She's had a shit life," I say. "She'd be in the Stress Center if she were rich. A lot of people here really should be in the Stress Center. She loves Damien, though. She's really trying to change for him."

Marianna closes her eyes for a long moment.

"Sometimes I wonder," she begins. "Do you think if we'd—"

"Don't even go there," I say. "I mean it. Do not go there."

"But Kyle's so desperately unhappy where he is, he's so angry about—" Marianna dabs at her red, swollen eyes, rocks almost imperceptibly in her chair as if trying to bring herself into balance. "I don't even *know* what he's so angry about. I'm afraid for him, Grace. I don't know how to help him."

Kyle would say, *It's her own fucking fault. Maybe she'll finally figure out how not to live like the world belongs to her.*

But Marianna had always been kind to me; she'd been kind to come here. She's not a bad person, just a clueless, well-meaning mother who loves her son. She's so used to everything going her way that there's a good chance it's never even occurred to her that what she wants me to do could get me into a world of trouble.

"Marianna," I say. "I can't help you with Kyle. You can't ask me to do that."

Her shoulders slump; every bit of beauty drains from her face. "I'm so sorry," she says. "I know. I know you can't help Kyle. And worrying about him is the absolute last thing you need right now. But are *you* okay? Are you going to be okay?"

"I'm doing what I have to do to get out of here. And I *will* get out."

Marianna's hands reach across the table, but I drop mine to my lap. Is it that she doesn't see the "No Touching" sign or that she assumes the rule doesn't apply to her?

"You're strong, Grace," she says. "You're so much stronger than Kyle. You're so good. It's just wrong that you're in a place like this. We all know that."

I hear the hard edge to my voice too late. "Because I'm better than the other girls here?"

"You are, Grace." Marianna shoots a quick glance at Jessica and begins to cry.

"No. I'm not. And I can't be with Kyle after I get out of here. Maybe he does love me, he probably does, and maybe I still love him, too, but I can't—" I pause, collect myself. "I just can't risk it."

"Okay," she says. "Okay. I understand. But you'll be careful."

"I'm careful," I say.

"Good," she says. "But do remember we all love you."

I nod, but I can't look at her.

When she's gone, the guard buzzes me back to the holding room to wait for an escort to take me back to Cottage Five. Sitting on the hard bench, I remember reading something in the artist's statement at the beginning of Marianna's book of paintings. *For an artist, nothing is lost*—her idea that art— the beauty of it—is made from everything that ever made you sad.

What will she make of Kyle's—and my own—stupid, willful rebellion, I wonder. What letters and words and parts of words, what colors and shapes, what almost-images will she use to capture and then obscure us?

Artist's Statement

Kyle was convinced that his mom purposely left groceries or artists supplies or whatever in her van and instructed the guard at the neighborhood gate to call her when Kyle and I passed through so she could hurry outside and pretend she'd just gotten there and ask us to help her carry the stuff in. "It's like she has a crush on you," Kyle said. "Like she thinks you're her daughter."

We'd carry whatever Marianna wanted us to carry up to the studio and she'd invite us to stay for a cup of tea. Kyle almost always said no. But once in a while—maybe he felt bad for being a jerk or maybe he was just in a good mood—he'd say yes. Sometimes he'd even tell her about something ridiculous that had happened at school or some weird person we'd seen at the coffee place or the movies, Marianna laughing, basking in his attention, and I could see how it must have been between them when Kyle was little. I loved being there, drinking my chamomile tea in the hum of their fleeting happiness, surrounded by Kyle's mom's paintings.

I'd look at them, one by one, as Kyle and Marianna talked. I fell into them, like falling into a story—only there was no story, just glorious color, with spiky black letters and letters and words and almost-words punching up through it, strung together, looping like concertina wire to make almost-sense. Sometimes like ghost words on an erased chalkboard, sometimes like part of a pattern of words left on a censored document.

Kyle hadn't told me his mom was a well-known painter. I only found out when I came upon a book of her paintings among the other art books on the big, glass coffee table. A catalog from a museum show of her work, Marianna said. She didn't say what museum, but the name of it was in the book—one in New York that I'd heard of.

"Would you like a copy?" Marianna asked.

"Yes, please," I said.

I kept the book in my backpack. I read and reread the artist's statement until I could recite it from memory: *For an artist, nothing is lost. All the joys and sorrows of life, the mistakes and indiscretions, the lives you might have lived, the people you might have loved, everything you long for, all you fear, all that will never fit in the life you finally chose (or chose you) find a place in your art. They are what art is made of.*

I loved looking at the paintings. Sometimes they seemed alive—changing to be what I needed at any given moment but never completely giving themselves up to me. Which made me want to look at them even more.

Could what Marianna said about art be true? I'd been too shy to ask her about it, so I asked Kyle instead. He said it was bullshit, just like everything else about his parents. Pure bullshit. Besides, what good did painting do in a fucked-up world? What's the point?

I didn't dare say, maybe the point is how making or even just looking at something beautiful makes you feel peaceful inside, filled up with light—and hopeful, even when you have no good reason to hope—because I knew he'd see my interest in Marianna's paintings as a kind of betrayal. I knew to keep my distance, despite Marianna's kindness to me. Despite the longing I felt to be embraced by what might be as close to a mother's love as I'd ever find.

Why Didn't You Tell Me?

The first thing Jessica says when I get back to the dayroom is, "Grace. Why didn't you tell me you had a boyfriend? Gosh, his mom is really, really beautiful, she looks rich, is she rich? Is your boyfriend, you know—does he look like her? What's he like? What's his name?"

"He's not my boyfriend anymore."

"Then why did his mom come to see you?"

I wave away the question.

125

"Did he break up with you because you had to come here, and his mom feels bad about it? I'm really, really sorry if that happened. But why didn't you tell me? You must be sad."

The whole thing with Marianna had exhausted me, and I *so* do not want to deal with Jessica right now. The third degree. The hurt, accusing tone.

"I broke up with *him*. I'm not sad."

"Does his mom want you to get back with him, then? Is that why she came?"

"Something like that," I say. "But I'm not *going* back with him."

The girls who saw me with Marianna are drifting in from their visits, probably thinking she was my mother. Some regard me curiously, some with hostile expressions. Some whisper to the girls who'd stayed behind.

"But Grace." Jessica persists. "How come you put her on your visiting list then?"

"I didn't. I don't know how she got on it."

But, of course, I know: another string pulled by some important person.

I also know Kyle asked his mom to come, knowing she'd have to suck up to someone to make it happen. Ha, I thought. He's just like her. I'd bet big money it didn't even occur to him that what he was asking for was just one more example of the kind of privilege he supposedly hates so much—until there's something he can't have without it.

Jessica sighs. "He must really love you a lot if he made his mom drive all the way from Indianapolis to try to talk you into going back with him."

"Yeah, well, in case you haven't figured out yet, love isn't all it's cracked up to be."

"You *are* hurt," Jessica says. "He did hurt you. I can tell. I'm here, Grace, if you want to talk about it—you know that, right?"

"Right. And—" The words burst from my mouth like water from a fire hose meant to disperse a riot. "*You* can tell *me* your mom is a meth addict, just like you."

Jessica flinches, as if I'd slapped her. Her face floods red.

But *Jesus*, it's her own fault, pushing, pushing the way she does, always wanting something from me that I don't want—can't afford—to give.

Still, I feel like an asshole. I am an asshole.

"I'm sorry, Jessica," I say. "I didn't mean—"

"No, I am." Her voice is so small. "I should have told you, but I hate where I come from, I hate what we are. I mean, my mom tries, but she's been a mess ever since my dad left, she didn't know how to take care of us, that's how she ended up, how we both—"

"I'm not going to be like her, though. I'm *not*. You watch. I'm going to take care of me and Damien. I wouldn't even put my mom on my visiting list except for if I didn't I wouldn't get to see him."

She's crying now. "I'm sorry," she says again. "I wanted you to think I was—better."

Which makes me feel even worse.

Multiple Choice

"This boy, Kyle, whose mother visited you Saturday," Dr. Welty says. "Tell me about him."

Of course, Dr. Welty would know who Marianna was. It's in my records. Everyone here knows everything. I shrug. "Men suck. That's pretty much all you need to know."

"You think of him as a man?"

"Hardly," I say. "So, okay. Boys suck. Whatever."

"But this one boy, Kyle. What attracted you to him?"

It's a goddamn multiple-choice question.

A. Nobody had ever paid attention to me like Kyle did.
B. I believed he really wanted to know me.
C. The headiness of going from being so good to being so bad. The liberation.
D. I was a bad person already, inside, and Kyle was a bad person, too. Naturally, I was drawn to him like a magnet.
E. He loved (loves) me.
F. Maybe just sex. Why not just sex?
G. Or the fact that sex with Kyle was so completely different from the terrible things Jack did to me.
H. All of the above.
I. Some sick combination of the above.
J. An answer that is not here, unknown.

"You were a good student before you met Kyle," Dr. Welty says. "You'd never been in any kind of trouble. Yet you're here for a serious crime—breaking and entering, theft—which could have landed you in real prison if the prosecutor had wanted to go down that path. I know Kyle's parents interceded and the prosecutor agreed to boarding school as an alternative to incarceration for him. I also know your parents did not attempt to intercede but, in fact, declared you incorrigible, which left the judge no real option but to send you here.

"Did *you* know this, Grace?"

I laugh, more of a bark, really, because I figure it's entirely possible that this was the first thing my parents had agreed on since their divorce. Then I'm crying, wailing really, pissed out of my mind that I can't control myself, can't stop, pissed at Dr. Welty for telling me the truth about my parents, which I've always known but until that moment had hoped maybe, maybe wasn't actually true, not totally true, anyway: they do not want me. They never, ever will.

I want out of here. I'd claw the door open, bound down the corridor, teeth bared if I could. I start to stand up, but sink back into my chair, not crying anymore, just shuddering. Dr. Welty hands me a box of tissues. I blow my nose, breathe. Breathe again, half surprised I can.

It's quiet for a long time, just the low hum of the fluorescent light on the ceiling. The red minutes on the digital clock slipping away. Dr. Welty regards me, her fingers steepled, her expression unreadable.

"Girls like you don't usually end up here," she says, finally. "They end up in therapy, for sure, maybe even in boarding school—like your friend Kyle. Maybe they get better, maybe they don't. I'm not saying that's what should have happened to you, that your behavior shouldn't have had the same consequences as the behavior of poor girls. I'm not even saying that because of where you come from you have a better shot at turning your life around than they do, which might be true—but there's no guarantee you'd accomplish it."

Shit. I feel like an antenna inside my head just tuned to a whole new station. Nobody has ever in my whole life said anything so honest to me; my body, all by itself, leans into her as she goes on.

"What I want to say to you, Grace—and I'll say it only once—is that in all my years of working with girls who have come to this place hurting and in trouble, the one single thing I know for sure is that the girls who make it are the ones who figure out it's a hard and lonely thing to *really* change your life, no matter where you come from. There may be people on their side who love and help them, or not. They may believe God is on their side and, if so, it may comfort them. But comfort is no substitute for, no assurance of a happy, productive life. In the end, no matter what you do to end up here, no matter what others did or didn't do to make you lose your way, no matter what you believe or don't believe in, you have to accept the fact that you, alone, are responsible for becoming who you want to be.

"So," she concludes matter-of-factly. "Kyle. We can talk about Kyle or not talk about him. We can talk about or not talk about your family. We can talk or not talk about—anything. But you will continue to see me once weekly as long as you are here, and I am one of the people involved in determining when you will be released. I don't mean that as a threat. Truly.

But I'd be irresponsible if I didn't say it would be good for you to think about that."

"Okay," I say, a bit dazed. "Yeah. I will."

Out in the Dead of Night, All Dressed in Black

"Smile, you look so pretty when you smile," this one guard is always saying, which pisses me off because One: I don't feel like smiling. Why would I? Plus, why would I want to look pretty for *him?* And two: There's no way he'd say, "Smile, you look so handsome when you smile," to a guy. A guy would punch him out if he said that, which is what I would like to do myself.

He's a creepy little twerp, wiry with a straggly black goatee and bulging Popeye muscles he hardens up and invites us to touch when there's nobody else around—which, just the thought of makes my skin crawl. Jessica thinks he's cute, but she doesn't smile at him—or anyone else—because of her meth mouth. You'd think she wouldn't talk as much as she does either, but meth mouth doesn't stop her from that. And what she talks about is how wonderful her life is going to be when she gets out of this place.

The first thing she's going to do is get whatever job she can and save up her money for new teeth. You can get all new teeth instead of getting your real ones fixed, she told me. They plug them right into where the old ones were. They're super expensive, but it's worth it. How else can she get a really good job so she can get her own apartment and a car and have enough money to buy toys and clothes for Damien and take care of him the way he deserves? Nobody's going to hire someone for a job like that with addict teeth, right? She doesn't care how much getting those new teeth hurts because it's for her future. Anyway, it can't hurt more than what's left of her real teeth now.

They're black with decay, some broken into pointy shards, some disappearing into her swollen gums. It makes me really glad I was smart enough not to go down that path—not that Kyle would have let me.

Once I'd completed his drug tutorial, the two of us smoked pot, we drank—that was pretty much it. Later, when things got all fucked up, stealing

130

became our drug of choice. Even now, considering where it got me, I feel higher than I did those few times trying party drugs just remembering what it was like to be out in the dead of night, all dressed in black.

It was such a rush the way the world shifted into slow motion as we sprinted across someone's backyard in moonlight, our long shadows moving with us. Then the deep quiet of an empty house, the exhilaration of stealing things we knew people treasured. The bliss of not caring that what we were doing was wrong. Not caring about anything.

EIGHT

Star-Crossed Lovers

Jessica begs me for details about Kyle. "Did he give you presents?" she asks. "I bet he gave you lots of presents." Ever since she found out about him, she's been working up a major fantasy about our relationship. "Star-crossed lovers," she says, sighing. She loves the sound of it, so dramatic, and refuses to believe it when I tell her star-crossed means doomed to fail.

"You and Kyle will be together," she always says. "I've prayed on it. I know it."

Once I said, sarcastically, "Okay, fine. You can be the bridesmaid."

At which point, Jessica's plain face became luminous with joy.

And I could hear Kyle's voice in my head: *Seriously. People who don't get jokes should be shot. Why don't you just tell her to fuck off. She's not your job.*

He was always telling me I wasn't responsible for making anybody happy but myself.

Once, not long after we got back from spring break at his parents' house in Montana—the beginning of that terrible, lost time that ultimately landed me here—I pointed out that he expected his parents to make him happy. That wasn't the same thing, he said. Parents are supposed to do that. It should make them happy to make their kids happy.

But when I said when Briony was happy, I was happy, too, Kyle said, "Listen. The thing is, Grace, you're going to have to cut your whole fucking family out of your life if you want to survive. What have they ever done for you—even your sister?"

"Briony *loves* me," I said.

I totally expected him to say. "Okay, you're right. Not Briony." But a hard look came on his face. "I love you," he said. "I give you everything. Isn't that enough?"

It wasn't. I would never, ever stop loving Briony. I couldn't. Which I didn't say to Kyle because it was exhausting to argue with him. Plus, he was upset, we both were. Surely, he knew in his heart that I had more than enough love for both him and my sister.

What Kyle Gave Me

- An iPhone with unlimited service
- A Wonder Woman t-shirt
- An amethyst mala bracelet for aligning the chakras
- A Tibetan prayer bracelet
- A silver necklace with a peace symbol
- A framed photograph of himself at eight, wearing a way-too-big, Indiana Pacers jersey
  - ("Life was perfect then," he said.)
- An iPad loaded with playlists of his favorite music
  - Bose headphones for listening to them
- Butterfly earrings
- A 'Don't Forget to Be Awesome' stainless steel water bottle
- An 'Amazing Grace' t-shirt

- The chaos tattoo
- A hoodie of his I said I liked
- A red North Face ski jacket
- (Almost) a baby

Nobody's Business

"What's the matter with you?" Electra asks. "Jeez. Speed up a little, would you? I'm not even breaking a sweat."

We're walking the track in the Shape Up Zone, but I can barely put one foot in front of the other. "I can't," I say. "I'm too tired."

"Girl, you've been all fucked up since that woman came to visit. You're not thinking about—" Electra stops, grabs my arm.

"No way," I say. "I'd never do that to my sister. Besides, weren't you paying attention during orientation? Offing yourself is against the rules."

Electra snorts, but doesn't let go until I swear I'm telling the truth.

"Did you ever?" I ask, when we start walking again. "Think about it?"

"Hell no," Electra says. "I was too pissed. My mom and her idiot husband, number four, get killed in a car crash, both of them drunk. No insurance, no grandparents, one aunt in bum-fuck Iowa who says she can't afford me, not with her being a single mom raising four kids of her own. She's really, really sorry. Right? And who the fuck even *knew* where my dad was. But I was thirteen, I figured it wasn't all that long and I'd be through high school and on my own anyway. A few years with foster parents, how bad could that be?

"Ha," she goes on. "A revolving door of complete and total assholes—and worse, starting with good old Lloyd. I can't even remember how many times I ran away. In the summers, I'd stay down under a railroad bridge in a tent I stole. That wasn't that bad. Like Girl Scouts, you know? Only with no stupid green uniform. I'd steal food, I'd panhandle in the evenings. I'd hang out in the library, reading, which I actually loved." She grins. "In case you wondered, that's how I got so smart."

"Good to know," I say.

"Yeah, well. I couldn't sleep there, so winter sucked. There'd be a sweep and I'd end up back with some family determined to improve me. Fuck that," she says. "I never *once* thought of killing myself. I wouldn't have given them that satisfaction. But you did, didn't you, Grace?"

"Yeah," I say. "I tried once. I don't think I really meant it, though. Maybe I just wanted to see if anybody cared."

"And?

I shrug. "They called my mom. It scared her, that's for sure. My dad still doesn't know. She didn't tell him because I got hysterical and said if she told him he'd tell Marlys and I'd probably never get to see Briony again. I guess that's a kind of caring."

"Maybe," Electra says. "But it's totally pathetic. I'm never having kids, I mean it. I'd just mess them up, and there's no way I'm going to do that to somebody."

"I almost did" I say.

"Almost did what?"

"Have a kid.

Electra stops short. "Whoa." she says. "Seriously?"

"Yep." I give her a little shove to keep us moving. "Last winter. I don't really want to talk about it right now. Just—when Kyle's mom visited, she started crying and said maybe the abortion, which she and his dad talked us into, was a mistake. Maybe we wouldn't have ended up in so much trouble if we had the baby."

"That *bitch,*" Electra says. "Like you really need to start second-guessing yourself about that, especially here. What is *wrong* with people?

Honest to God, that's why I decided I want to be a shrink: to figure it out, you know?"

Really? That's really what you want to be?"

"Yeah," Electra says. "What? You think I'm not smart enough?"

"No. Not at all. You're *totally* smart. It's—"

"What? I'm a fucking criminal, so who's going want me as their doctor—even if I could afford to go to college? Which I can't," she adds, bitterly.

"You *can,*" I say. "You're too smart not to go to college. You can find a way."

"Right. And that way is—?"

"I don't know," I say. "I just believe in you. You'll figure out a way."

For once, Electra is quiet.

Then she says, "One thing I do know: It was nobody's fucking business what you did about that baby but your own. You *should* be pissed at Kyle's mom, at all of them."

"And that's your professional opinion?"

"It is." Electra grins. "I'll send you the bill."

It's a Wonderful World

Lauvette's man—as she calls her boyfriend, Dante—keeps her commissary account topped off, and she shares the food she buys with Kenyae and Jasmine: popcorn and chili they microwave in the dayroom when it's allowed. They talk endlessly about their friends and families, complain about the TV shows they're missing because there's no cable here, the white trash food they're forced to eat in the cafeteria, and how they're not allowed to braid their hair but have to keep it natural, in a short afro. The way they laugh and carry on, you'd think they were at a sleepover instead of locked up in prison.

They make me think of Kyle and me navigating around the groups of Black girls laughing and talking in the midst of the stream of other cliques making their way to class in the crowded hallways of our high school. It got edgy, sometimes there were fights between groups, but mostly those girls were exuberant and completely unselfconscious in a way I wished I could be. I envied how they owned whatever space in which they found themselves.

I remember going to Briony's kindergarten graduation: every kind of kid—White, Black, Latinx, Asian—lined up on risers singing, "It's a Wonderful World." Their high, fluty voices, their sweet earnest expressions had hurt my heart. I was twelve at the time and, already, the Black and Brown girls who'd been friendly in elementary school had begun to pull away and become a universe in their own right; kids had begun to sort themselves out in ways that left others standing outside their circles. By high school, I had to be so careful in so many different ways that, before I met Kyle, the only time I felt really safe was when I was by myself. Which is how I wish I could be here, even though, lately, I'm so lonely I could die.

I tell myself it's just depression. I've been depressed before. I know this feeling of moving through the day like I'm trapped in an impenetrable block of glass. Wishing I could cry because it would be a relief, but I can't because you have to feel something to cry and I don't feel anything at all. It was how I felt after the abortion, after I tried to kill myself. It scared Kyle. The harder he tried to make me feel better, the worse I felt—until the night he texted me an hour or so before picking me up: *Wear your black hoodie.*

I figured we were going to the paintball place again, where dressing in black gave you an advantage because it helped you fade into the shadows. Which wouldn't be the worst thing. Moving through the paintball landscape in the heavy equipment mirrored how I felt anyway, made it feel normal. And I liked the sense of purpose I felt, concentrating on my prey. I liked the feel of the paintball gun in my hand, the satisfying burst of color when I hit my mark.

"Admit it," Kyle said, after the first time we played. "You feel better."

I did, though only for a little while.

137

But that night it wasn't paintball Kyle had in mind.

"Payback time," he said, when I got into the Jeep.

"For—?"

"Everything. Everyone."

"Meaning?"

"You'll see," he said.

He'd been pissed off, fierce for weeks. That night he was almost mellow. We drove around a while, stopped for frozen yogurt, then turned onto a dirt road that led to some woods near the reservoir. He parked and we made out for a while. The sweet, slow kind of making out, like in the beginning.

At midnight, he got two black baseball caps and two black pillowcases from the back seat. He put on one of the hats, pulled his hood up over it, then gave the other to me. When I did the same, he pulled the strings so you could hardly see my face. He gave me one of the pillowcases and a pair of gloves, the kind doctors use.

I wasn't stupid. I knew what the black pillowcase and the gloves meant. But I got out of the car and followed him anyway, down a dark path toward an enclave of expensive houses I could just barely see through the trees, my heart pounding, scared shitless.

More awake than I had ever been.

Kyle stopped where the woods ended, at the far edge of someone's backyard. "I know them," he said. "They're on vacation. So, Amazing Grace, are you ready?"

I took a deep breath and said, "Yes."

We took off running toward the house. Kyle found the key in a fake rock among the shrubbery, as if by radar. "Morons," he said. "Fuckers deserve to be robbed."

He opened the back door. We stood there a long moment until we were sure there was no alarm, nobody there, then entered through the kitchen. Kyle tapped the flashlight icon on his iPhone to lead our way. In the study, he took the silver letter opener from the surface of the desk. Rummaging through the drawers, he scored several gold pens and a wad of cash.

I opened a curio cabinet in the living room and took one of the ceramic cottages displayed there, one of the little ceramic boxes, a rabbit contemplating a fat carrot—Limoges, I knew because Marlys collected them. Kyle took two silver candlesticks and a family picture in a silver frame.

We didn't go upstairs that first time. We got in and got out fast, leaving the door open behind us, streaking across the back yard and through the woods, holding in our high fives and shrieks of laughter until we were in the Jeep, bumping our way back to the main road.

Kyle said it wouldn't be right to profit from what we'd stolen, so he drove downtown, where we tucked bits of the cash into the belongings of homeless people sleeping on park benches or the grass. We put the silver candlesticks and the silver frame, the family picture removed from it, in a Goodwill box at a nearby mall. Later, in Kyle's bedroom, we smashed the Limoges box and the little cottage because people just shouldn't value stupid shit like that.

It was absurd how many people left their homes virtually unguarded when they went away. Kyle kept his ears open for information about people going on vacation: a classmate from the private school he'd gone to, some friend of his mom's or business acquaintance of his dad, a retired couple in his neighborhood. We started staying in the houses longer, taking more— heirloom jewelry in worn velvet pouches, antique sabers, Faberge eggs. Once Kyle made us sandwiches with ham and cheese he found in the refrigerator, and we sat down in the kitchen and ate them like we had all the time in the world.

There was no name for the mixture of terror and exultation I felt, sneaking around in a dark house, searching for the right combination of valuable objects to drop off at Goodwill—a different store each time, always in a poor neighborhood. Treasures for people to find, the kind of things the owners of the houses would value in the most personal way: family photos, trophies, keepsakes, just one piece of an expensive collection probably assembled over years. The bitter pleasure of dumping the breakable treasure on his bed like Halloween candy, then letting it slide to the floor, where we'd shatter it with hammers, grind it beneath our boots. All I knew was that in those months when Kyle and I were stealing, I felt utterly and completely alive.

And here I am, paying for it now, in a state of depression so dark, settled so deep inside me, that I can't make myself believe it will ever go away. Winter setting in doesn't help. The cold gray days, the wind that whips right through my flimsy jacket as I walk in line, hands behind my back, to the cafeteria, the Shape Up Zone, the Promise Academy. It's freezing in the dayroom, in the classrooms. Barred windows slice the ugly brown grass, the skeletons of trees, the silver snippet of river into squares.

My body clenches against the cold, only releasing in the warmth of Dr. Welty's office. The mug of hot tea I hold in both hands might be the most exquisite pleasure I've ever known. Since Kyle's mom's visit, words have begun to pour out: the divorce, my parents, Marlys, Briony, Kyle. Not Jack, not the almost-baby. I'm not prepared to share that kind of shame with anyone, not yet, not even Dr. Welty, who listens and occasionally asks a question that startles me and stays in my head, agitating.

> *Do you think your mom might actually have wanted to divorce your dad?*
>
> *Do you think she just doesn't know how to love you? Or anyone?*
>
> *Do you think Marlys might be insecure?*
>
> *What do you think your dad hoped his marriage to Marlys would be like?*
>
> *What do you think Kyle saw in you that you couldn't see yourself?*
>
> *Do you think your mom and Kyle's mom have anything in common?*
>
> *What do you think Briony misses most about you?*

Do you know anyone without some kind of longing?

Volunteers

"Christmas is for poor people," Electra says. "The time of year when people feel sorry for you, clean out their cupboards and give you food they don't want, and chip in at work to buy crappy stuff they think you need. Then forget you again.

"Though, okay, once I got a Barbie Dreamhouse. I put it on my list and I got it. I was like, seven. Who knows why some person decided to do that? Of course, the next year whatever I put on my list—I don't remember what it was, just that Santa *didn't* bring it, and I was crushed. I figured it was because I was bad. After that, I didn't want anything to do with Christmas. If people tried to give me stuff, I'd just say, no thanks.

"Have you had the volunteers yet?" she asks me.

"What volunteers?"

"You'll see." Electra raises her arm to show off the new yellow wristband. "Get ready."

They descend upon Cottage Five the second Saturday in December: three Kiwanis volunteers with Christmas craft supplies and cheery determination. Professional women, Ms. Stephanie says when she introduces herself, Ms. Elizabeth, and Ms. Lauren. She's an insurance agent, Ms. Elizabeth owns a dress shop, Ms. Lauren is a lawyer. They're all wearing Christmas sweaters. Ms. Elizabeth's earrings are tiny blinking Christmas bulbs, one red, one green.

Excellent role models for us wayward girls.

They live in the town just outside the fence. They love working with the Kiwanis Club, whose motto is "Serving the Children of the World."

"Not that you girls are children," Ms. Stephanie says, with a smile meant to win our hearts. "But we do care about you and hope to make a difference in your lives."

I duck to hide my smirk. I don't know what Electra did to get the yellow bracelet, but there's no question whatsoever about why.

Ms. Elizabeth glances at Wren, who's on her couch, reading as usual. "Honey, won't you join us?" she asks. "We have some lovely projects for you to do."

Wren ignores her.

"She doesn't, um—" Jessica says. "She's—"

"Batshit," Amber mutters.

Ms. Stephanie takes a deep breath. "So. How about if you girls introduce yourselves and we get started bringing a little Christmas cheer to this place?"

Every girl, but Wren, says her name. Ms. Stephanie repeats it.

"Lovette," she says when it's Lauvette's turn.

"LAWvette," she corrects.

"Lovette," Ms. Stephanie says again.

"Forget about it," Lauvette mutters. "Just keep my name out your mouth."

Ms. Stephanie flushes.

Jessica, the last in the circle, jumps into the prickly silence with her name. "And thank you all so much for coming," she adds. "I just love Christmas. I can't wait to do the crafts. I have a little boy, Damien. He's almost two. Do you think I could send him something I make?"

"Well, I don't know." Ms. Stephanie glances at Officer Franklin, who takes Officer Hadley's place on the weekends. She's reading her *People Magazine*, as usual, and doesn't look up. "We'll see what we can do about that."

"Thank you," Jessica says. "Really. Thank you so much for coming."

At which point, Ms. Stephanie assigns her to Ms. Elizabeth's table, not her own.

"I love your earrings," Jessica says to Ms. Elizabeth. "They're so cute. Do you have kids?"

Ms. Elizabeth rather anxiously admits that she has two daughters, four and six.

"Oh," Jessica says. "They still believe in Santa Claus! That's so great. I'll bet they're excited. My Damien is too little to understand, you know? But next year, he'll be three. That's the best time, I think—and I'll be there with him. But my mom and my aunt are taking him to the mall to see Santa this year anyway. They promised to send his picture. I just hope he's not scared. Last year he cried. He didn't understand about Santa. He was only one.

"Do you want to see a picture of him?" she asks, taking the creased picture of Damien in the fire truck from the pocket of her khakis.

Amber groans.

"Oh, my. What a cute little boy," Ms. Elizabeth says—then resets herself, assumes a professional expression and gets the crafts session back on track.

There are five projects to choose from: paper-plate angels, paper-plate wreaths, construction-paper Santas, popsicle-stick Christmas trees, and paper chains. Ms. Elizabeth lays out the supplies for decorating: glitter, cotton balls, markers, stickers, tiny bows, glue. The pieces are in Ziploc bags, cut and ready to put together because, of course, no scissors.

Outside the window of the day room, snow is coming down so hard that the tree line is just a haze. You can't see the river at all. If you could get out of this place and run, the snow would fill up your tracks so fast they'd have a hard time finding you. On the other hand, you might freeze to death. It hasn't occurred to me until this particular moment to be pissed off by the fact that it's impossible to know how warm or cold it is outside. Would stepping out into the snowy day make me feel gloriously alive, like that day, skiing with Kyle, or would it feel like a slap in the face?

I watch Jessica, bent over a set of three Popsicle sticks, coloring them with a green marker, serious as a kindergartner. When she's finished, she applies the sticker ornaments, then Ms. Elizabeth helps her brush the glue onto the ends to create the triangular Christmas tree shape. She brushes more glue along the front and hands Jessica a bottle of glitter to sprinkle on it. Last is the yellow sticker star for the top.

Jessica beams, reaches for the construction-paper Santa.

Briony could have done a better job on any one of these projects when she was three.

I pick up a bag with red and green construction paper strips in it, mindlessly glue them together, thinking about making paper chains with Briony, how I tried to guide her hands to press the ends together when the strips wouldn't stick together right—and Briony's indignant response: "Self!" She always said that when people tried to help her. "Self." I loved that so much, at least partly because it drove Marlys absolutely wild. But if you left her alone, Briony would almost always figure out how to do whatever she was trying to do.

Lauvette's voice startles me back to the present. "No brown Santas here," she says. "Just all these pink ones. What's that about?"

"We ain't *down* with making pink Santas," Kenyae says.

All the other girls look up, except for Jessica, who concentrates even harder. Now she's working on the paper plate wreath, putting red dots on it from a whole sheet of them. Ms. Elizabeth glances at Officer Franklin. Still reading.

The women exchange anxious glances. "I'm so sorry we didn't think of that," Ms. Stephanie says, handing Lauvette a brown marker. "But! You can make the face brown yourself!"

Lauvette takes it, she has no choice, and scribbles the pink face brown.

"That is *just* beautiful," Ms. Stephanie says.

Lauvette rolls her eyes.

The three women exchange glances again and I can see them decide it's time to wrap up the crafts and move on to the cookies and juice—which they do with impressive efficiency. Though Kaylie spills her cup of juice into Destiny's lap (intentionally, I saw her do it, saw her sly grin), then grabs a handful of napkins, drops to her knees, and uses them to sop up the juice from Destiny's crotch, both of them giggling madly.

This, finally, gets Officer Franklin's attention. She sets down her magazine, walks across the rug that defines the no-man's land of the guard desk past the pathetic fake tree awaiting our newly made ornaments to grab the two of them by the backs of their shirts and haul them away to their rooms.

"I'm so sorry," Jessica says, near tears, as if she'd misbehaved herself.

Ghost of Christmas Past

As Christmas nears, Officer Hadley gives each of us two Christmas cards and two stamps. She bought the cards and stamps herself, she says. Everyone should be able to send holiday greetings to their families. I ask if I can give my cards and stamps to Jessica and she says yes.

"You're sure you don't want to send at least one of them to your family, though?"

"No, thank you," I say.

"Well," she says, a flicker of sadness crossing her kind face. "I'm sure Jessica will be glad to have them."

An understatement. You'd have thought I'd given her the key to a brand-new car.

"Thank you, *thank you*," she says. "Now I can send one to my grandma, too. And an extra one to Damien, one for each of his sweet little hands. I just wish you had some family you wanted to send them to, though. I really do, Grace. Are you sure there's no one? What about Kyle?"

"Especially not Kyle," I say. "I told you—oh, never mind."

I rue the day Jessica found out about him. Never, ever will I let it slip that I got a Christmas card from Briony. I still haven't told her I have a sister. She'd want to know every single detail about Briony and carry on about how unfair it is that Marlys and my dad are keeping us apart. No, thank you. I certainly didn't tell Jessica I got a Christmas card from them. Jesus, Prince of Peace embossed in gold on a scarlet background, and inside:

In celebration of the One who is everything

Have a wonderful Christmas and a Blessed New Year

Really? I thought. Here?

It had a printed signature: Bob, Marlys and Briony Lowery.

I tore the card into the tiniest possible pieces and flushed them down the toilet. I wasn't going to think about them, or about my mom, who I haven't heard from once since I've been in this hellhole. But I can't stop thinking of my Nana, those long-ago Christmases when she was alive. And missing her, though she's been gone for almost as long as I can remember.

Nana loved Christmas. The day after Thanksgiving, the two of us would drive to a Christmas tree farm out in the country, pick the perfect tree, and load the trunk with branches for the fireplace mantel. Then we'd go back to Nana's house and turn it into a Christmas wonderland. She had boxes of decorations, some for the tree, some for all over the house—even the bathrooms. There was a special box with my favorite ornaments in it—some Nana had bought me, some that were my mom's favorite ornaments when she was a little girl. Every year she gave me one of those calendars with little glittery doors. You opened one door each day of December and there was a tiny picture of an angel or children playing or maybe a toy—and on the very last day, Christmas Eve, the baby Jesus. The first thing I did every morning was open the door for that day; then I'd call Nana to tell her what the picture was, and Nana would say, "Oh, my goodness! That sounds just splendiferous!"

She was small and skinny, her curly white hair cut short. She looked nothing at all like you'd think Mrs. Santa would look, but she dressed up like Mrs. Santa on Christmas Eve anyway, in a red dress with white fur on it, and peered out of the window and said things like, "Oh, dear. I do hope there's plenty of snow for the reindeer!"

One year, I asked, "Is Santa my grandpa?"

Nana laughed so hard her face got bright red and she scooped me up and hugged me and said, "Sweetie, I'm just pretending. You know your Grandpa is in heaven with the angels. But let's pretend Santa really is your grandpa, and you get every single thing you want."

"A dog," I said. "That's the only, only thing I want."

I felt my mom's mad eyes on me, felt the happy drain from Nana's body, and I burrowed deeper into her shoulder and held her tighter because we both knew my mom was going to say no dog, not even if Santa himself delivered it, and I should have known better than to mention it. Santa brought me a stuffed dog every year, though. I named each one and lined them up on my bed and slept with them every night. Later, after my dad went to live with Marlys and I visited him there, Marlys said they were so grubby I could only bring one at a time.

There was one good thing about my dad going to live with Marlys: my mom let me spend Christmas Eve with Nana—and even stay all night. I didn't have to worry about Santa not knowing where I'd be because I told him when Nana took me to see him at the mall. Nana took me to night church, too, which I loved because the church smelled like Christmas and there were tall white candles at the end of every pew and beautiful singing and when we came out into the cold night, the sky was black, with twinkling stars. Back at Nana's, we snuggled together in her bed. She was so warm; she smelled like cookies.

Nana never met Marlys and I was glad of that because I didn't want Marlys to have a chance to be mean to her. Once Nana had asked in a worried voice, "Honey, is Marlys nice to you?" I said yes. The truth would have upset her. Plus, I was being as good as I could be when I went to my dad's house because I still believed Marlys would start to love me.

Nana's Box

Nana died when I was six. I cried so hard when my mom said that meant we would never, ever see her again because I loved Nana so much and Nana loved me—she said so all the time. But the next day my mom and Aunt Marjorie took me to a big house, and there was Nana, sleeping in a box in the living room.

I was so happy. "Mom," I said. "Look! Nana's here. But why is she in that box?"

"Hush, Grace," she said. "Not now." And she and Aunt Marjory kept crying and hugging each other.

When I asked Jack, he pretended like he didn't hear me and walked away.

I stood on tiptoe and whispered to Nana, "Why are you in the box?" But she stayed quiet. She didn't smile at me or raise up her arms for a hug. She didn't even look like Nana; she looked like a big doll of Nana. I wished I was big enough to pick her up and tip her backward so her eyes would open like a doll's eyes did, so Nana would see me and smile and tell me what she was doing here.

I sat quietly, the way my mom liked. I had new shoes that were black and shiny and I raised them up and lowered them and moved them sideways watching how the light moved on them and how, if I held them really still, they were like little black mirrors and I could see things in them. I had a new dress, too, but it was scratchy and also I didn't like the color of it, which was gray instead of my favorite color, yellow.

The living room of the house was a lot bigger than our living room and there were a lot of flowers in it. The whole room smelled like flowers, but not the way flowers smelled outside, more like Aunt Marjorie's perfume that made my stomach hurt sometimes when I was sitting on her lap. The flowers were very pretty, though, and I walked along counting the bouquets. I was up to thirty-two when Jack came over and kneeled down by me and smiled and wrapped me in his arms and I breathed in his smell, better than flowers. I didn't care that the jacket of his suit scratched my face.

"You're being such a good girl, Grace," he said. "I'm very, very proud of you."

This time he answered my question about the box. "It's a special box for people who die," he said, then picked me up and carried me to where Nana was. "See? It's like a bed. Because dying is like going to sleep. You just don't wake up, that's all, and so you need a soft, beautiful place to sleep forever."

The box *was* beautiful: shiny white, with gold handles, like the kind on drawers, and pink material in the top of it, like a bunch of tiny pillows all stuck together. Nana's head rested on a special pink pillow, and Jack tipped me so I could touch it and feel how cool and soft it was.

"See," Jack said. "Your Nana is very peaceful. Her body stopped working and went to sleep, but her heart is alive and it floated up to heaven. She's an angel now, watching over you."

More and more people came and looked at Nana and hugged my mom and Aunt Marjorie. Some cried and said how sad, what a lovely person Nana was, she's in a better place now, in the arms of God.

After a while, Jack said, "You must be getting hungry, honey. I told your mom I'd take you get some dinner. Shall we go now?"

First, he had to get gas, though. After he put it in the car, he opened the door on my side and said, "I have to go to the bathroom, and I don't want to leave you here all alone so you can come with me."

He locked the door, then set me on the counter next to the sink. I didn't look when he went to the bathroom, I knew you weren't supposed to watch when people did that. Instead of helping me down when he finished, he put his hands on my shoulders and looked at me and his eyes got all wet and shiny. "You're such a good girl," he said. "I love you very much. Do you love me?"

I nodded.

I did love Jack. He played with me and tickled me and carried me on his shoulders sometimes. He brought me presents—pretty barrettes for my hair and Barbies and, once, a sparkly yellow shirt. He was always nice to me and said how pretty I was and never once yelled or made me feel bad. Now he pulled me against him and rubbed circles on my back and it made me feel sleepy and good. When he tilted my face up and lightly kissed my lips it felt like he was tickling me, but inside, and I kept my face there so he would do it again.

Back in the car, he asked, "How about ice cream for dinner?"

"Yes!' I said.

So, we went to Baskin Robbins and had chocolate ice cream with extra sprinkles on it and Jack laughed and said, "Yum, yum. Doesn't this chicken and broccoli taste good? Would you like another helping?"

I giggled. "Yes! More chicken and broccoli!"

So, he got me some more ice cream and watched me eat it, smiling.

When I was finished, he wet a napkin at the water fountain and wiped the chocolate from my face so, so gently it felt like he was kissing me again and he said, "This is our secret, just you and me, right?" and put up his hand for me to high-five him and I did.

NINE

S.A.D.

Ms. Miller props a poster on an easel in the dayroom where we've gathered for the first group session in January: a gray background that looks like snow is falling on it, just like the day framed in the window, and a depressed snowman in the bottom-right corner, his coal mouth turned down, his carrot nose askew, his black eyes turned-up crescent moons, his brown stick arms raised to his temples as if to massage them.

At the top: "Seasonal Affective Disorder."

It's a kind of depression that comes and goes based on the seasons," Ms. Miller explains, then reads the symptoms listed on the poster aloud:

Feeling depressed most of the day, nearly every day.

Feeling hopeless or worthless.

Having low energy.

Losing interest in activities you once enjoyed.

Having problems with sleeping.

Experiencing changes in your appetite or weight.

Feeling sluggish or agitated.

Having difficulty concentrating.

Having frequent thoughts of death or suicide.

"Seasonal Affective Disorder," she concludes. "S.A.D."

"SAD," Lauvette says. "Fuck, yeah, we SAD. But sad don't need no season here."

"Language," Ms. Miller says, but Lauvette ignores her.

"Depressed. Yeah. Every single fucking day."

"Low energy. Try no energy," Amber says.

Lauvette goes on. "That losing interest thing, though? Not a problem. I got interest. Problem is, no what you call them—conjugal visits?—in this damn place. I'd be way better if I can get me some, you know, with my man once in a while."

"Girl," Jasmine says. "You right about that."

Bree barks out a laugh.

Kaylie and Destiny exchange a meaningful glance.

"Girls," Ms. Miller says, blushing. "Please."

Amber and Maria giggle.

Then laughter catches us all, like a wildfire.

"Sad," someone will say when it starts to die down, igniting it again.

It feels good, laughing. I can't remember the last time I laughed like this, so hard my stomach hurts, so hard I'm almost crying. Even Ms. Miller is laughing, for once living in our world, seeing us, *really* seeing us living in it. Maybe that's why Lauvette reins us in and settles us down to the task.

"Just look out there right now," she says. "All gray and ugly and cold. Who ain't gonna be depressed?"

"And we got crappy coats," Amber chimes in. "Talk about sad. Like they don't even care we're always freezing."

"And no scarves for covering up our faces, either," Maria says.

"Ha," Kenyae says. "'Cause they think we'd hang ourselves or maybe strangle each other."

The laughter threatens to start up again, but Lauvette gives them the evil eye. If she were a good girl, teachers and counselors would say she had "leadership qualities." Plus, she's wicked smart, anyone can see that. If she cared about school, she could easily be first in any class.

Like Kyle, I think.

"If he would just apply himself," Mariana always says. "He could do anything. Be anything." If Kyle ever did anything at all he was supposed to do she'd act like he was a genius. Which would only piss him off and make him more determined to be a slacker.

What is Lauvette refusing to care about, I wonder? What, exactly, is she rebelling against? She's not only smart, but even dressed in the hideous clothes we're forced to wear and no makeup, she is beautiful—a creamy brown, with high cheekbones, almond eyes with just the tiniest slant to them, full lips the color of cranberries. She moves with this sexy insolence, anger coiled tightly inside her like the figure inside a jack-in-the-box, just waiting for the turn of a handle to release it.

She says when she gets out, she's going to move to California, where she'll find a rich man who wears beautiful suits and silk ties and smells like expensive cologne. He'll marry her and buy her a house and she'll make everything in it pink and gold. There'll be a spa and a swimming pool and a little bell that all she has to do is ring it and a maid will come out and ask, "Miss Lauvette, what can I bring you?"

"I'll say, you know, champagne, filet mignon—" She waves a hand, laughs. "Taco Bell. And she'll run right out and get it for me."

What's wrong with wanting that? Kyle would ask. *If you believe women have the right to choose what to do with their lives, who are you to judge?*

153

I don't disagree with Kyle—who's not even here, I remind myself. But a part of me feels like it's a sad thing for a woman to want, especially someone as smart as Lauvette. If she'd had a different, better life, would she still want that?

I feel Kyle shrug inside me.

As for my own dream: a happy family, a sense of belonging. How pathetic, how lacking in imagination is that? Not to mention the fact that Lauvette's dream of marrying a rich man who will take care of her and give her everything she wants is a whole lot more likely to come true than my dream of life with Dad and Marlys morphing into one of those cheerful blended TV families that makes a place for everyone and takes shopping trips and spa days with me.

And how had my fantasy of becoming part of Kyle's family been any different? To be loved by them, given every opportunity, rewarded for every accomplishment, no matter how small. "They don't even fucking know me," Kyle said more than once when I told him how lucky he was to have parents like that.

Now, suddenly, I see how he was right.

Worse, he'd become addicted to their money and power, using them in ways that made him feel unworthy and ashamed. No wonder he was pissed off all the time. I get what he meant when he said the great thing about drugs is how they make you just not give a fuck about the things that upset you and make you sad.

Life is mellow, more beautiful on drugs," he said. "If you're listening to music, it's like the music is happening inside you, the notes running up and down your nervous system, floating in your blood. You're not here. You're in some whole other zone of being."

I see him in my mind's eye, his sly smile impossible to refuse.

Open your mouth, he says.

I do.

He places a tablet of ecstasy on the tip of my tongue, puts his arms around me, and draws me down to his bed, where we lie for who knows how long, blissful, the only two people on the planet.

Better Living Through Chemistry

Kyle looked at drugs like a science project, like each one was a hypothesis to prove. He believed it was an obligation to experience the far ranges of reality in human existence, to search until you found the perfect drug for *you*: the one that gave you the best high with the least unpleasant or possibly disastrous consequences. He kept a handwritten log, where he recorded his research and reactions.

I said, "If you worked this hard in chemistry class, you'd be getting an A."

"Like I care about that," he said. "I want to learn what *I* want to learn. Not what some geek chemistry teacher thinks is important."

As far as I could tell, except for Fentanyl, Kyle had tried pretty much everything, including heroin, which he told me made him purely happy. It was *awesome,* he said. The trouble was if you got hooked on it you were toast. So, he checked it off the list and left it at that.

Same with meth: the rush to end all rushes. It went on and on. The problem was it made you obsessive: as in he couldn't stop washing his Jeep, sometimes twice a day—inside and out. Like, what if you got obsessed with something dangerous? Plus, meth made your teeth rot and then you looked trashy.

LSD: Whoa! Far out! But it could fry your brain. All you had to do was look at those old, burned-out hippies for proof of that.

Speed: You feel like the freaking captain of the universe. Until you're an asshole who can't sleep. Plus, suuuper addictive. No, thanks.

Cocaine: Same, more or less. Snorting, you had to do it, like, every twenty minutes to keep it going. Smoking crack made you mean and crazy.

Ecstasy: Well-named! A very excellent rush, followed by a calm that made you feel you had every single thing you ever needed and more—and it would never, ever go away. No big deal to take it once in a while, if you were careful.

Magic mushrooms: They were natural substances, which was always better. And spiritual. One more thing indigenous people got right. You had to watch out, though. Dealers fucked with them sometimes, and you could get more than you'd bargained for.

Marijuana: You should smoke it regularly for no other reason than the fact it was still illegal in so many places, which was stupid and wrong. It was no worse than having a few beers, and what about those bougie wine drinkers, like his own parents, who acted like it wasn't like real drinking because wine was so *civilized*. Not to mention, way more people died from smoking cigarettes than smoking a joint now and then. And grass gave you a sweet high. Did you ever see anyone get obnoxious when they were stoned?

Kyle couldn't believe I hadn't tried anything—except for beer, which I'd sneaked a sip of once when I was a kid and thought it tasted terrible. Kids were drinking at parties in middle school, but I never did. I didn't like the idea of getting out of control and doing something I'd be embarrassed about later. Then, after Zoe traded me in for Monica, I didn't get invited to parties anymore. I spent weekends by myself, reading, or with Briony, when I was allowed to go to my dad's house. It was fine with me, really. I didn't like parties anyway. I'd go from feeling like a grotesque parade balloon that everyone was gawking at to a cockroach, skittering toward the safety of some unnoticed corner.

I wonder now what in the world I was thinking when I let Kyle talk me into experimenting with drugs, how I let him convince me he'd be a reliable guide—though I have to admit he sort of *was* reliable. As reliable as anyone could be under such circumstances.

"I'll be your spotter," he said. "You know, just watch, until you get your drug legs."

Which he did, in his room over the garage.

Of course, I liked getting high. Duh. Who wouldn't?

"No shit," Kyle said. "In grade school, they're always getting you to make those 'Say No to Drugs!' pledges when you don't have a clue what you're saying 'no' to. Then you get woke and give it a try and you're, like, *never mind*. The truth is, they don't want you to feel that good. Plus, FYI: I happen to know that my parents keep a stash weed in the safe in their bedroom."

We went through the list, one by one—and Kyle's personal research was mostly right. My LSD trip was not all peace and love and rainbows like his had been and he had to talk me back from a forest so dense that all I could see were trees hemming me in, dripping with blood. Plus, coke scared the shit out of me because it made me feel I could do anything, be anything (anyone) I wanted to be.

Our default was grass: easy to get, lovely to lie in Kyle's bed, stoned, giggling and bingeing on Doritos or Twinkies. It was like this for more than a year, always just the two of us. I'd never been so happy—and maybe because being happy made me need my family less or maybe because Kyle came from a "good family"—things got a little better with my parents. And Kyle's parents, especially Marianna, treated me like a beloved daughter.

In time, we might have grown up, gotten married, and lived happily ever after.

It could have happened that way.

Really. It could have.

A Better Person Than You Are

Maybe it's S.A.D., maybe I'm catching a cold. I can't tell. When I felt this bad last spring, I thought I had the flu that was going around school. I threw up constantly. Once I looked in the mirror and—seriously—my face was green. Kyle skipped school with me and the two of us holed up in his apartment. He made me drink water and orange juice and fed me crackers that I threw right back up again. Almost two weeks passed, and it still didn't go away. I'd missed a period, but my periods had always been irregular, and I told myself it was the same thing now.

Besides, I couldn't be pregnant, Kyle always used a condom. But after the third week, I went to the drugstore by myself and bought a pregnancy test just in case—and the pink line appeared. As if all the throwing up had been my body shouting, "Yoo-hoo! Pay attention! You're having a baby!", the vomiting stopped, and I began to feel better.

"I was getting scared," Kyle said. "I was about to make you go to the doctor."

I should have told him right then, but I didn't. I felt paralyzed, weak. I was so tired that once I fell asleep in the middle of having sex.

"Are you okay?" Kyle kept asking until, finally, I said, "I'm pregnant."

"Shit!" he said. "We always used—"

"I know. I don't know how it happened. I'm sorry."

He gently raised my head and said, "I love you, Grace. What should we do?"

His parents were the ones who decided.

We were simply too young to have a baby, they said. Our lives would be ruined if we went ahead with it. There was no way we were ready to take on the responsibility of raising a child, and if we gave the baby up for adoption, we'd never be able to forget that it was growing up somewhere, with people we didn't even know. Plus, how could we be sure those people would give it the right kind of life or even be good people?

If they thought about the fact that if the baby was born it would be their grandchild, neither of them mentioned it.

"Have you told your parents?" Marianna asked. "Can you tell them?"

"No," I said. "I haven't. I can't."

"Then we'll take care of you," Marianna said.

They had a ski chalet in Montana—a state where underage girls didn't need their parents' permission—and I could go along on their usual spring break vacation and have the abortion there. Nobody would ever have to know.

She put her arm around me and drew me close. "I'm so sorry you have to go through this," she said. "But you do see that abortion really is the only choice here?"

I did. It was no good dwelling on my realization that believing in pro-choice, which I did, absolutely, turned out to be a whole lot more complicated when you actually had to choose. Not to mention trying to stop me from imagining the baby who'd be born if I didn't stop her: a girl as small and sweet and real as Briony had been the very first time I saw her. But all I had to do to reassure myself was imagine what my parents and Marlys would say if they found out.

Now, in the circle of sad girls, I can't get the thought of the almost-baby out of my mind. And the fact that if I hadn't had the abortion, Kyle and I never would have done the stupid shit we did. I'd be taking care of a baby instead of being locked up in this place. And so what—Kyle might not have turned out to be the best father in the world, but he'd never have abandoned me. His parents would have taken care of us; they'd never have let Kyle suffer. They'd have loved the baby, too. How could they not when it was made partly of him?

It. A baby is not an it. But there's no other way I can think about this because I'll never, ever know who that baby would have been. After the abortion I just wanted to get away from the clinic as fast as I could. It was done. Fuck it. Time to move on.

Now I'd give anything to know.

Afterwards, I was bereft. Kyle was enraged. He wouldn't or couldn't say why. Was it as simple as being pissed at himself for doing what his parents wanted him to do? Or was it that, for the first time, ever, his parents' determination to solve his problem hadn't made him feel happy, at least for a little while?

When I asked if he was mad at me for getting pregnant in the first place, tears came to his eyes. He wrapped me into his arms. "No," he said. "No way. It wasn't your fault. It was nobody's fault. It happened. I just hate what you had to go through because of it, how much it hurts. I don't want you to be hurt. Ever. It kills me, even to think of it. You know that, right?"

"I do," I said. "It's okay. It didn't hurt that much. Really. And it's over."

But it was as if somebody had to pay.

Which, ironically, turned out to be me. But that wasn't Kyle's fault. It really wasn't. It wasn't as if I hadn't participated fully in the spiral of destruction in those months after the abortion, it wasn't as if I hadn't taken my own pleasure smashing what I knew was valuable to the people we stole from.

Guilt is why I can't make thoughts of the baby go away. It's why Jessica's constant monologue about Damien only makes me feel worse. At least she had the courage to have him. She might not be smarter than me, but she's for sure a better person than I am.

Face it, I tell myself. Even your fucking mother is a better person. She didn't even want kids but she didn't kill you .

This is crazy thinking, I know. But I just can't get it out of my mind that what I stopped from growing would have become a baby made of Kyle and myself. A tiny being who would have been born loving us, who would have needed our love and protection the way I still yearn for love and protection from my own parents.

No doubt, Kyle and I weren't ready. We'd probably have made a big fat mess of things. Most people do, as far as I can tell.

I can't go back and change it. I just have to move through the chaos.

Your Body Belongs to You

Here at the Wabash Valley Juvenile Correctional Facility, there is zero tolerance for sexual abuse and a lot of talk about how your body belongs to you. If anyone touches you in an inappropriate way you have permission to pick up the unit phone, punch in #33, and report it. Which is the last thing anyone with a brain in her head would do because, fine, staff is trained to deal with it, but what about when they're finished dealing with it and you're back on the unit and whoever touched you or hurt you is still there, too.

And what about when a guard almost does it, but not quite, like grabbing your upper arm and pulling it in so his hand presses against the side of your breast or holding your hair at the back of your neck like a lover might do just before a kiss, or just staring at you, his hands in his pockets and, if you look, you can see him getting hard?

What are you supposed to do about that?

Nothing. Or figure out how to keep them distracted.

I used to do that with Jack. He liked to watch me reading, so I'd sit in my special reading chair, my nose in a book, knowing he'd sit in his own reading chair, his hands in his lap, his mouth a little bit open and his eyes not quite right—and leave me alone. Or if he did come and scoop me up and take me to the special bedroom it would just be to lie together with his arms around me, whispering what a good girl I was and how much he loved me. Sometimes, even when I was way too big for it and I could read perfectly well myself, he'd say, "Sit on my lap and I'll read to you." I'd pretend to fall asleep on his shoulder and, if he kissed the side of my face or my hair, I'd give little sigh and nestle deeper. Usually, when I did that, he sighed, too, and didn't wake me.

From nowhere a memory floats up: a first-grade worksheet with a picture of a boy and girl wearing bathing suits. "Your body has private parts on it," the teacher said. "They are the parts covered by your bathing suit."

A girl raised her hand. "Your vagina is one," she said.

161

I didn't know what that was, so I was sorry when the teacher said, "Yes, it is. But we're not going to talk about those words today." She told us to take out our crayons and color the worksheet and, when we were through, she said, "Let's practice what to say if someone touches your private parts without your permission. Does anyone have an idea of what to say?"

"Say, no! Don't touch me there!" the vagina girl said. "Then tell your mom or dad."

"Yes," the teacher said. "Very good. It's important to tell your parents if something like that happens—or another grown-up you trust."

When she gave us a blank piece of paper to draw someone we trusted, I drew Jack. He loved me more than anyone and always listened to me and he took care of me at Jack Camp. He never, ever touched my private parts then. I touched his.

At first, I was scared. It was so ugly. But Jack said, "Don't be scared, this is the part of a man's body made for love. It gets big when a man loves you."

Like his was.

He didn't ask me to touch it the first time, just look at it while he touched it himself and it got even bigger and he said, "See how much I love you?"

Then he put a towel over it and closed his eyes and shivered a couple of times, like he was cold, and when he took the towel off it had shrunk and curled up like a fat worm—which, he said, was what it looked like when it was waiting.

I'm furious when I think about this now. At Jack, of course; at my parents because they should have been paying attention; but, mainly, *still,* at myself for believing it was love—and I have the same damn argument with myself I've had a million times.

But how was I supposed to know?

I used to be afraid that someone would hurt Briony the same way Jack hurt me. I'd glare at the neighborhood men who were friendly to my sister. I'd do the same thing when my dad and Marlys had company, until Marlys said I was being rude and sent me up to the bedroom—which I was glad for because Briony always insisted on going up, too, and that meant she was safe.

The thing is, though, Briony is the least cuddly, least needy kid I've ever known. Even when she was a really little girl, if either of my parents made the mistake of ruffling her hair or patting her on the shoulder, Briony would narrow her eyes and make her chirpy little voice fierce.

"No touchin' the body!"

It cracked me up every time, but it made Marlys furious.

If Marlys opened her arms and said, "Give your mama a hug," Briony would duck under them and run away. If Marlys caught her and wrapped her arms around her, Briony stood stiff as a Barbie doll until Marlys let her go. She was utterly, gorgeously confident in her independence. A man like Jack would see right away that there was no way she'd be susceptible to his so-called love.

This is one of the few things I'm sure of, and I'm grateful for the knowledge—not least because it scares me to think what I might do to anyone who even tried to hurt my sister like that.

Cleaning Day

Belle cleaned Jack's house from top to bottom every Tuesday. It was my favorite day of the week. I had a key to his house because I always got to Jack Camp before he did, but I didn't have to use it on Tuesdays because Belle was waiting for me on the corner when I got off the school bus. We'd walk the block to his house, me telling her about my day, and when Belle opened the door there would be the smell of the peanut butter cookies she had baked for me, my favorite kind. She'd pour me a glass of milk, put some warm cookies on a plate, and set it down in front of me.

"Honey," she'd say. "You eat."

Then she'd sit down next to me and we'd talk some more about what happened at school that day and about Belle's grandchildren. Sometimes it made me feel jealous the way Belle was so proud of them, how the words she used praising them sounded like a song. But she praised me, too. She was so proud of how I got one hundred percent on every single spelling test and never, ever got anything below A's on my report cards.

I wished Belle could come every day, not just Tuesday, because then Jack would stay late at school every day and, when he got home, he'd have to drive Belle to her house down in the city and there wouldn't be time for him to take me to the special bedroom.

When I was nine, I asked Belle if I could come and live with her.

"Oh, sweetheart," Belle said, "I wish you could. But it wouldn't be right for me to take you away from your family and Mr. Jack."

I almost told her then. I almost said, "My parents don't love me, and Jack hurts me when you're not here." But I was afraid Belle would think I was lying.

"Please," I said. "I wouldn't miss them, and I could still visit whenever they wanted me to. I'd just live with you and sleep at your house."

Belle looked sad. "Honey, I've got a houseful already, you know that. All those children and grandchildren still under my roof. There's not a bit of room for anyone else."

I didn't ask again, but Belle started looking worried when she met me at the school bus on Tuesdays. I felt her watching me sometimes. I felt bad for making her worry and tried hard to be good, helping her with chores in the kitchen, drawing pictures for her to take home to her grandchildren. But Belle just seemed to get sadder.

Then one Tuesday, we got to Jack's house, which, like always, smelled of cookies, and Belle made me a plate. But when we sat down at the table, Belle said it was her last day. She wouldn't be working for Mr. Jack anymore. She was too busy with her own family.

I couldn't help it, I started to cry. "No," I said. "Please don't go. You can't."

"I'm sorry, honey." Belle looked like she might cry herself. "I'm so sorry. But I've got to take care of my family. I know you understand that."

I nodded my head, yes, I understood. I didn't want to hurt Belle's feelings or make her worry more. But what I really understood was that I had loved Belle too much, needed too much from her, and that was the real reason she was going away.

TEN

Sick Pass

I've felt like crap for days—just a cold, but I keep feeling sicker instead of better. And I'm so tired I feel like I'm going to die. On my way to my appointment with Dr. Welty, I stumble after Officer Snap, lightheaded, nearly falling when she gives a little shove to hurry me up the stairs.

"You don't look well, Grace," Dr. Welty says at the sight of me.

And, of course, I start crying.

She leans toward me. "Grace? Has something happened to you?"

"No, I'm fine. Really. It's just, I have this stupid cold. Or I don't know, maybe it's a sinus infection because every time I blow my nose this gross gluey yellow stuff comes out. Sorry," I add. "Like you need to know whatever gross stuff is coming out of my nose."

Dr. Welty laughs, which surprises me into a blubbery smile.

"There. See?" Dr. Welty says. "It's not so bad."

"What," I ask. "The gross gluey stuff or my life?"

"Hmmm," Dr. Welty says. "That's for you to say, isn't it? Though you do look a bit peaky. Do you have a headache?"

I nod. I've had it for days now, little knives behind my eyes. My head feels full of cotton balls, my ears ringing, probably because I'm constantly blowing my nose. Four whole boxes of Kleenex so far—the only thing other than shampoo and deodorant I've allowed myself to buy from the commissary since I got here. All I want to do is sleep.

Dr. Welty reaches across her desk, brushes my forehead with her fingers, a gesture that makes me go liquid inside. It's been so long since anybody touched me like that, gently, not grabbing or pushing like Officer Snap does when she's sure nobody's watching.

"You're burning up," Dr. Welty says. "I'm sending for the nurse to take you to the infirmary right now. We can talk next week."

I've been trying so hard to suck it up and pretend I'm okay that I start crying again, though tears just leak from my eyes—as if they're as tired as I am. I fold my arms on Dr. Welty's desk, put my head down, and the next thing I know I'm propped up on fluffy pillows in a real bed in a real room with sunlight streaming in through an unbarred window.

There are other beds in the room, but they're empty. Through the doorway I can see a nurse in a starched white uniform working at a desk. Am I in a hospital? No—because I can see the high fence from my window, barbed wire coiling along the top. There's a handmade card on the table next to me, just a folded piece of paper with a heart on the front, "Get Beter Soon." I open it. "I miss you and Im praying for you. Your frend, Jessica."

Oh, God. Jessica. I sigh, vaguely remembering her fussing over me, making my headache worse, when I just wanted to sit in the dayroom with my eyes closed until I could go to bed. Sometimes I think Jessica will follow me back into my real life, talking until the moment I finally, blessedly take my last breath. She'd follow me to heaven, still talking, if I believed in it. Which makes me smile, prompting a surprising moment of fondness for Jessica—in the abstract. The thought of actually being back in the dayroom with Jessica makes me close my eyes in exhaustion.

I open them, who knows how much later, to the nurse bending over me, wiping my forehead with a cool cloth.

"Well, there you are." The nurse smiles. "I was beginning to wonder."

"How long have I been here," I ask.

"Three days," the nurse says.

"I've been sleeping three days?"

"Yep. Pretty much. A bit of flu on top of that nasty sinus infection—and a big hit of antibiotics that knocked you out good. So. How do you feel?"

"Better," I say. "I guess."

"Good," the nurse says. "Are you hungry?"

"Yes." Suddenly, I'm starving.

The nurse brings real tomato soup, a real grilled cheese sandwich, a Coke in a glass with ice in it. Later, she brings a cup of tea, with lemon squeezed into it.

By the next day, when Dr. Welty stops in, I'm starting to feel like a human being again. "Could you just give me a sick pass for the rest of the time I'm here?" I ask, trying for a joking tone, but not quite achieving it.

"Believe me, I wish I could," she says. "I wish I could put every single one of you girls in a better place. I really, truly do."

"Why do you *work* here?" I ask, then apologize for my rudeness.

"No worries," Dr. Welty says. "It's a good question, a worthy one, and I'm going to give you an honest answer: 1) because I care about you girls and 2) because I'm curious about what the world does to a girl that makes her end up in such a place, how you girls manage here, how—whether you can learn something that might make a difference when you leave.

"Of course, I'd like to be someone who makes a difference," she says. "It's why I got into this kind of work in the first place. And it does happen sometimes. But it's not enough, it's not why I stayed. If it weren't for curiosity, working here would break my heart."

Girl Crush

"Oh, my gosh, I missed you, Grace," Jessica says. "I really, truly did. It scared me *so much* that you were sick. I mean, like, do they even have real doctors here? I prayed on it. I'm so glad you're better."

"Thanks. And for the card. That was nice."

"I wish I could've got you a real one," Jessica says.

"It's okay. It's nicer that you made it."

I still feel weak, I still have a dull headache, and I still want more than anything to sleep. I long for the infirmary, where it was quiet, where the nurse was kind to me. Where there were real pillows and food that didn't make me gag and I could lie in bed and read or just look out of the window and watch the snow fall. Where I could think—

About what Dr. Welty had said about being curious, about how being curious instead of scared or depressed or pissed off all the time—if I could even manage it—might change me. About Kyle—how he loved me and how it had gone bad and how I can't afford to take another chance on him, but what am I supposed to do when I can't make myself forget him?

And Briony, whose letters have come every week since that first one in December.

Ordinary stuff, Briony's life is blessedly ordinary—if privileged— with its tight schedule of ballet and piano lessons and horseback riding and who knows what else. She'd tucked her fifth-grade school photo, wallet-sized, into one of the letters and I look at it whenever I can, even though it's impossible to see it without tears springing to my eyes, without praying, even though I don't believe in prayer, *Please let her always be this way.* Open, shining. I can't look at it without thinking of my own fifth-grade photo, the time with Jack barely over, still showing in my hunched shoulders, my worried face.

If I could sign up for the worst kind of flu, any awful disease that would send me back to the infirmary, I'd do it in a heartbeat. For the rest of my life, Cottage Five will join Jack as the stuff of my worst nightmares, I'm sure of it. And coming back feels like starting all over. The airlessness of the dayroom, the constant buzz of tension that seems like a living thing, the other girls needling me when nobody is watching.

"Hey, rich girl. You been on vacation?"

And, of course, Jessica's already getting on my last nerve.

She's speaking in her usual, maddening run-on sentences about how her grandma brought Damien to visit Saturday but her mom didn't come with, and she doesn't know why, she promised she'd come after the new year because she couldn't come in December, she didn't say why then, either, the thing is, you know, it's a long way and her grandma coming alone worries her because the two of them usually take turns driving and keeping Damien occupied, and what if her grandma had an accident?

"You should see him," she says. "He's getting so big. And he can draw! Some ladies from the church came and helped with the little ones so, you know, the grown-ups could visit, and one of them helped Damien. It was so cute, he was concentrating so hard, holding the crayon in his little fist.

"He said 'car,' clear as anything, when I asked him what it was. Then he said, 'Go. Ride.' He's getting so many words, I'm so proud of him. I remind my mom and grandma all the time to read to him, so he'll get even smarter.

"You should come to fellowship on Monday nights," she segues. "Those same ladies come and some others, too, and there's refreshments. It's real nice."

"I don't think so," I say. "But thanks. Anyway, we need to get to work on your math...I've got a lot of homework to catch up on because I was sick."

"Okay." Jessica sighs. "I really hate math, though. But I know I have to do it."

I scoot her chair closer so we can both see the page of problems.

Amber saunters by. "Aw, look at Jessica," she loud-whispers. "Happy now her girlfriend's back."

Kaylie and Destiny giggle and make kissing sounds.

"She's not my girlfriend," Jessica says. "She's my friend. She's helping me with my homework."

"Yeah, yeah," Destiny says. "But we know what you're doing with your foot under the table while she's doing your math. Moving it up to that *place*."

"I am not," Jessica says, near tears. "I wouldn't do that. I would never—it's a sin to do things like that. It's wrong for girls to be that way together."

"Aw, man," Amber says. "Little Miss Jesus Loves Me. Everybody knows you've had a girl crush on Grace ever since she came. I bet you pray on it every night." Her voice goes high and trembly. "Dear Jesus, please, please save me from the sin of pussy love."

"Cut it out," I say. "Leave her alone."

Amber grins. "Oh," she says. "The butch. The manly protector."

"Fuck off," I say, my voice low but fierce. "Fuck the hell off, all of you."

Then, suddenly, I'm dizzy, I can't quite see right, and later I can't remember the impulse to pick up Jessica's math book and hurl it toward Amber, then the Chutes & Ladders game Jessica had claimed from the bookshelf to play when our homework was done, the board flopping open, the cards and plastic game pieces scattering everywhere, and my voice, screaming, "Fuck you fuck you fuck you! Fuck this whole goddamn fucking place!"

Until I'm down, Officer Hadley holding my hands behind my back, a sorrowful expression on her face. Because she's a decent person, she cares about the girls in Cottage Five, she wishes us well, and now I've royally fucked up and made her have to call Officer Snap to haul me away.

Solitary

I hesitate at the threshold of the cell.

"In," Officer Snap says, with a little shove, and I stumble in. I feel her in the doorway, feel her satisfaction in having cause to bring me to this place, but no way am I going to turn around to acknowledge it. I lock my throat to keep from begging. *Please. Don't leave me here. Please. Don't.*

"Think you're better, don't you?"

I shake my head.

"Look at me," Officer Snap says. "You turn around and look at me."

I turn.

Officer Snap's piggy little eyes, her stubby freckled hand on the taser at her hip. She's vibrating with malice. "I knew you'd end up here the day they brought you in," she says. "So full of yourself, like your shit don't smell. Well, get over it. And just so you know: Nobody cares much what happens here, nobody's really watching." She pushes me into the cell. "Remember that and maybe you'll get out in the time they gave you. Forget it, and you'll be spending quite a while in this deluxe room. It's up to you."

It's up to you. If one more person says that, I swear to God I'll—what? Which is why it makes me so fucking mad when they say it. Because nothing is up to you in this place. There's nothing about your life that is your own, nothing you can control, nothing you want that you can have.

But wait, Kyle would say. *You wanted to get the hell away from Jessica, you wanted just one day without her fawning all over you, blabbing on and on about Damien and the fabulous life they're going to have when she gets out, and you her only friend in the universe—and now you have three days.* He'd grin. *You just should have been a little more specific with the cosmos about what that would look like.* But I'm in no mood for irony.

I'm so pissed off I don't even realize Officer Snap is gone until the slice of light from the door disappears and I hear the click of the lock. Then I'm terrified. The room is the size of the walk-in closet in Jack's house where

I hid sometimes. There's a bed, no mattress, no pillow, just a scratchy army blanket folded at the foot. There's a toilet, a sink. Cement block walls, linoleum floor, a single light bulb in wire mesh on the ceiling. Breathing slowly, deeply, too calm myself, I inhale the smell of unwashed bodies, the coppery smell of menstrual blood. I taste vomit in my throat and swallow it back, gagging.

Three days. How will I even know?

Night and day are exactly the same here.

The Apartment

I made a pretend apartment in the closet in the special bedroom room at Jack's house. I went there when I was feeling sad and sometimes when I hurt in my between-the-legs-place from what Jack did to me. Sometimes I cried, but quietly so Jack wouldn't hear.

One day an imaginary friend came to the apartment. Her name was Cathy. She had blond hair and she always wore a blue scarf I thought was beautiful and wanted for myself. But Cathy wouldn't give it to me. She said it was all she had because she went away from her yard, which she was never ever supposed to do, and now her mom didn't know how to find her. Or maybe her mom didn't want to find her because she'd been bad.

I said, "Don't worry. Your mom wants to find you because moms always want to find their girls." But I just said it to make Cathy feel better. I didn't really believe it.

In the apartment, Cathy and I played Mother and Daughter and took turns being the mother and the daughter. It was the same every time. The daughter cried and cried and then the mother found her and took her in her arms and said, "Don't be sad. I will never, ever let you get lost again."

One day Jack was mad. I didn't know why, and I went to the pretend apartment to hide from him. Cathy was there. He called, "Grace, where are you?" But I didn't answer. Then he yelled it, "Grace! Where are you?"

"Grace, come on. Let's play Mother and Daughter," Cathy said.

"No. SHHH. Be quiet."

But she wouldn't be quiet. She started being the daughter and whining about being hungry for a treat and Jack heard her. The door opened. He had his wolf face on.

"Get out of there," he said. "Stop that crying."

But Cathy wouldn't stop and that day he took Cathy instead of me. He grabbed her arm and dragged her out of the pretend apartment and slammed the door but it bounced open again so I could see. He kept saying, "Stop that crying, stop that crying," but Cathy didn't stop until he put his hand over her face and she couldn't cry anymore. I knew what that felt like, I knew he was squeezing Cathy's mouth hard so she couldn't make a sound except inside herself, which hurt really bad but not as bad as what he did after, which was the same thing he did to Cathy the day he took her instead of me.

I watched even though I didn't want to because it was gross what he did and there was blood and after that he took Cathy to the bathroom and washed her but I couldn't see that part, I only heard Cathy still crying.

"Don't cry, don't cry," Jack said but it wasn't his mad voice anymore. He said, "Be a good girl now, I love you."

Electra's Voice

"So, Miss Best Behavior, what did you do to end up here?"

Electra.

"Hey. Grace. I know you're here. I was watching through my teeny-tiny window when Princessa Snap shoved you in the cell. In case you're too wigged out to notice, you've got one, too. On your door. I'm looking out mine right this second. So, get up off the so-called bed and look through yours and—*voila!* A deep human connection, just what we need in these times of trouble. Ha. Ha.

"Or you could pretend we're having a special group session with Ms. Miller, *sharing.*

"Okay," she says, when I don't answer. "Fine. Keep wigging out all on your own. FYI, There's nobody here but us. Nobody gives a shit if we talk our heads off, which is pretty ironic since they're scared shitless of us talking when we're supposedly being good. So, come on. We're good till they drug us up for the night. What did you do? Seriously. I'm getting a kick out of thinking about you acting up. I'm dying to know the specifics. I, personally, beat the shit out of somebody who totally needed the shit beat out of her. Fucking bully. Somebody had to do it, right?

"*Grace.* Come on. Are you okay?"

"Yes," I say. "No. I'm not. I'm—"

"Are you hurt? Did that bitch hurt you?"

"No. I'm just—"

"I know. The first time here is pretty awful. But it's not really all that bad, once you get used to it. It's quiet. Okay," she says when I don't respond. "If you won't tell, let's try multiple choice. You A) beat the shit out of somebody who also totally needed to have the shit beat out of her, B) got caught palming your meds, C) talked in line—and kept talking even when reprimanded, D) got caught having mad, passionate sex—

"Um, let's see. E) murdered Princessa Snap? Wait. Scratch that. I saw her deliver you here with my own eyes.

"Wait! Now I've got it. E) verbally and with great vigor rejected the Core Belief and Guiding Principle of Hope."

That makes me laugh. It feels good. "F) Totally lost it," I say. "Went totally berserk in the dayroom."

"Whoa!" Electra says. "Over what?"

"Pretty much everything," I say. "It was very freeing. For about two seconds."

"Yeah, well, good for you. You've needed to explode for weeks."

"Bullshit," I say. "How do you know what I need?"

"I'm psychic, remember? Besides, I know," Electra says, "because I'm one of those people who knows. And you know exactly what I mean because you're one, too."

"And what is it we supposedly know?"

"That nobody's going to take care of us," Electra says. "Not here, not anywhere. Not ever. You can play by the rules, but it only makes you weaker. It sucks away your soul. And don't pretend you don't know what I'm talking about because another thing I know is when someone's lying. This shit is not going away."

"What shit?"

"You know that, too. Whatever happened to you, whatever some asshole pervert did to you is not going away. Because he's here right now, isn't he? The pervert. And he never goes away. He doesn't have to, he's not afraid. He knows you're not going to tell on him, he knows you think it's your fault what he did. And he knows that, even if you do tell on him, they'll put you through so much hell that you'll end up worse off than if you'd kept your mouth shut—and he'll just walk away.

"You know what I'm talking about, right? I know you know."

"Okay, yeah. I know."

"And you know nobody really gives a shit."

"Yeah. I know that, too."

Electra falls silent.

I can feel Jack hovering near, dark and malevolent.

"Electra," I say. "*Electra.*"

"I'm right here."

"I *can* feel him. Like he's right here, even though I know he's not."

"Yeah," Electra says. "What I do—wait, what's his name?"

"Jack," I say. I can't even remember the last time I said his name out loud. I said it all the time when I was little. Jack, read me a story. Jack, can we swim? Jack, I want a cupcake. Jack, Jack, Jack, Jack, Jack.

He always said, yes. He was the best person in the world to me after Nana died, the only person who tried to make me happy when I was sad. How could I have said no to him?

I feel him come closer and I curl into a tight ball, pretend to be asleep like I used to do. That was mostly when I was older, when he was nearly finished with me, when I knew that what I let him do to me was wrong but didn't know how to make him stop. It made him mad if I tried.

"Pretending to sleep is the same thing as telling a lie," he'd say, "and I think you know lying is wrong." And I did know lying was wrong, so I opened up to him, though sometimes I did it crying.

When he broke up with Aunt Marjorie, my mom told me it was because Aunt Marjorie wanted to get married and Jack said no. But I knew it was my fault. Jack was mad at me because my girl parts were changing, and he thought they were so gross he stopped loving me and stopped being Aunt Marjorie's boyfriend so he'd never have to see them again. Aunt Marjorie cried and cried when he said it was over. Her heart was broken, she was so lonely. Jack didn't even want to be her friend or my mom's friend, either—and no more Jack Camp. Which made my mom furious.

"Never count on a man for anything," she said to Aunt Marjorie. "I've told you again and again and you don't listen. Where do you think I'd be right now if I hadn't figured this out after Bob went off with Marlys? Why do you think I nearly killed myself to pass the real estate test so I could make enough money to never, ever need a goddamn man again? To hell with Jack. I'll send Grace to a sleepaway camp this summer and not have to worry about her at all, even if it costs a fortune."

I didn't want to go. I asked my dad if I could stay at his house in the day and help Marlys take care of Briony. But Marlys said no, I'd just be in the way. Then I asked my mom, "Why can't I just stay home by myself? I'm almost eleven. I know how to fix my own breakfast and lunch: I could pretend it was school and stay inside and practice math and read library books. I won't go out at all, I promise."

But my mom said no, I was too young and, besides, she knew me. More likely I'd pretend I was an abandoned orphan and cook up some crazy story and scare myself half to death and go running next door to Mrs. Avery's house like I did that time she'd stepped out for just a minute.

I said, "But I was only seven then."

My mom said, "Enough! You're going."

And that was that.

"Hey!" Electra says. "Grace. Are you still there?"

"Yeah. I'm here."

"Okay. What I do is just bring it on. My guy, well the first one, was my first foster father. Lloyd. Seriously, *Lloyd.* Who would marry a guy named Lloyd, even if he wasn't a pervert? Anyway. What I do is just say it over and over, which—especially in the case of Lloyd because it's such an intrinsically stupid name—eventually makes him seem ridiculous instead of the monster he really was. Oh, and thinking about the tattoo on his bicep that said, yes, 'Lloyd.' Like, what? If he forgot who he was he could check his arm? Assuming he could read.

"But Jack! There's a name you can work with. Jack off. Jack around. Jackass. Jack it up. Jackhammer. Jack the Ripper. Jack Robinson."

"Jack in the box," I say. "Jack of all trades. Gimme some Jack. No, wait. Gross. I take that back."

Electra hoots. "Yeah. Do it," she says. "Take it back. Take your self back while you're at it. He may have fucked you up good, but he doesn't own you. And neither does anybody else."

ELEVEN

Fellowship

We get points for attending Monday night fellowship, which is bullshit because what about the division of church and state? "You're right," Dr. Welty said when I complained, but encouraged me to go anyway— especially after the incident that landed me in solitude.

"If you can tolerate it," she said. "Girls go for a lot of reasons, you know. Some do believe, of course, but some just want a break from the usual evening routine." She smiled. "And there are refreshments."

So, despite the fact that Jessica will think it's my first step down the path toward salvation, I decide to give it a try, just sit there and zone out. I've done it plenty of times going to church with my dad and Marlys—but no. It turns out *fellowship* is a verb. The church people rise, beaming, when the twenty or so of us get there and motion for us to take a seat at one of the round tables. They greet the girls they recognize by name, welcome the rest of us with bright smiles.

"Miss Anna, this is my best friend, Grace," Jessica says to the woman at our table.

I shoot her a murderous glance, but Jessica blathers on about how I stood up for her in the dayroom and got in trouble for it, and how nobody else had ever done anything that nice for her before.

"I'm so grateful the Lord brought us together," she said.

Miss Anna, thin as a stick, with iron-gray hair pulled back in a bun, says, "We're all so glad you're here, Grace. Do you know the Lord? Have you taken Him as your personal savior?"

"She hasn't," Jessica answers. "Not yet. But I've told her about how He saved me, how sad and lost I was before I put my life in his hands, and I believe that Grace is going to find him, too. I pray on it all the time."

"We'll pray on it together," Miss Anna says. "He can make your time here so much easier, Grace. He can give you purpose that will see you through—forever."

"Yes, ma'am," I say, breathing against the impulse to bolt from my chair and beg Officer Snap, who's standing at the door, smirking, to take me back to Cottage Five. It's not like I expected church here to be like Marlys's church, where everyone's tastefully dressed and keeps their personal relationships with Jesus to themselves—except on their tote bags and license plates, of course. But I didn't expect to be accosted, either—though, considering Jessica's enthusiasm for Him, I probably should have.

Miss Anna goes on, "When Pastor Dean asked for volunteers to make a fellowship here, Jesus said to me, 'Go. There are girls suffering in that place, girls in need, girls longing to be loved and forgiven, girls who need my light. You can bring them to me.'—and I have. You can't imagine," she says, a goofy, star-struck look on her face. "Oh! To bring a person to the Lord—"

She's interrupted by the slick-haired Pastor Dean, who stands and raises his hands, palms-up, at which point everyone bows their heads for his prayer. It goes on awhile, about how we're all sinners, every single one of us, we come to the world in sin and all we can do is be warriors for God, finding forgiveness for our own sins by helping others, hating the sin but loving the sinners and believing they will find the right path.

I keep my head bowed. I always refused to do that when I was bullied into going to church with my dad and Marlys, but I can't afford to bring attention to myself here. I don't believe in God, I've never found a shred of evidence that He exists, and if He *does* exist—as Kyle was always quick to point out—He's got a whole lot of explaining to do. I keep my eyes open, though—a small rebellion—glancing from the handouts at each girl's place, to a rubbed-away spot on the table where somebody probably wrote or drew some kind of graffiti they'd tried to erase, to Miss Anna's bony hands, the thin, worn gold wedding band on the left one. I have to rein in a smile when I lower my gaze and see her shoes: black, with straps across the top that buckle on the side, like little girl shoes, except clunky, with thick rubber soles.

"Church-lady shoes," Kyle would call them.

After the prayer, Miss Anna asks a girl named Lori to read the Bible verse on the handout, and Lori stumbles through it:

"Do not be bound together with unbelievers; for what partnership have righteousness and lawlessness, or what fellowship has light with darkness, or what harmony does Christ have with Belial…"

"That's the devil," Jessica whispers to me. "Belial. Another name for him."

"…or what has a believer in common with an unbeliever. Second Corinthians 14-15."

Miss Anna allows a few moments of contemplation, then asks, "What do these verses say to you? What special meaning do they have in this place where the Lord has set you down to test your faith in Him?"

Lori says, "We should stick together? So we won't be tempted?"

"What tempts you here, Lori?" Miss Anna asks.

Lori blushes, the girl beside her snickers.

"Hate," Jessica says into the uncomfortable silence that follows. "Sometimes I hate, you know, the guards, the mean ones, and some of the girls when they make fun of me, when they say my little boy, Damien, is ugly.

He's not ugly." Her voice cracks. "He's beautiful, all babies are beautiful, God made them. Though he's not exactly a baby anymore, he's two. Anyway. I ask Jesus to help me forgive them, but He doesn't, I can't—"

Touching is strictly forbidden at the Wabash Valley Juvenile Correctional Facility, except, apparently, at fellowship, because Miss Anna puts her hand on Jessica's, and I have to look away from Jessica's hungry expression, the way she turns her hand up so the lady can hold it, their fingers intertwined.

"He will," Miss Anna says. "I promise you, He will. In time. And isn't that the test, no matter where we are: to keep our faith, to keep believing, to pray on top of our wrong feelings until His light comes and fills us to the brim and there's no room inside us for anything but that.

"To stay among believers," she goes on, releasing Jessica's hand. "Second Corinthians tells us this, 'Do not be bound together with unbelievers.'"

"But—" Jessica glances at me, then at Miss Anna, who nods at her to continue. "What if your best friend is an unbeliever, but she's a good person? And sometimes there are believers who are mean. What about that?"

"Then they are not true believers. They are not true warriors of God."

"But my friend—"

Miss Anna smiles, but it's a fake smile, and her voice a this-is-the-end-of-the-conversation voice. "Then you must bring her to the Lord. It is our duty as Christians to bring the ones we love to Him."

Jessica looks stricken.

There is no way I'm going to be brought to the Lord and there's no way I'm going to fake it—even if I could. I'd like to snap Miss Anna's skinny neck. I hope the woman has granddaughters who will turn out to be heroin addicts or, worse, atheists, and end up in this godforsaken place. Okay, I don't really hope that, but I'm furious with myself for not realizing that by deciding to come to Fellowship I was setting Jessica up to fail in her Christian duty—

one she believes she must fulfill if Jesus is going make her dreams come true. The look on her face right now reminds me of when Briony figured out Santa Claus wasn't real.

There are refreshments, as promised: cookies that taste like cardboard, two on a napkin for each girl, and sweet tea with no ice. We sing the hymn printed on the handout: "How Great Thou Art." Then we recite the 23rd psalm, also printed on the handout, which I recite along with the others until they get to *"Yea, though I walk through the valley of the shadow of death,"* when my voice stops working and I feel, actually feel, that dark shadow fall upon me.

The Opposite of Belief

"Sucka," Electra says when I tell her I went to fellowship.

We're in the Shape Up Zone, walking the track, keeping an eye on the proctor, who, luckily for us, is more interested in refining her jump shot than fulfilling her duty to harass anyone trying to have a conversation.

"Don't worry," I say. "I'm not going back. I knew it was bullshit, but I thought maybe I could put up with it. Get some points back after solitary, get the hell out of here."

"What's *bullshit* is that going to fellowship has anything to do with when you get out," Electra says. "It's wrong. It ought to be illegal. In any case, forget about sucking up to those people. You've got too good of a crap detector to be any good at it."

"Yeah, well. The trouble with a good crap detector is if you can't ever turn it off you're mad at pretty much everything, pretty much all the time."

"And? That's a problem because—?"

"It's exhausting," I say. "Unless you're *Kyle*. He has a way better crap detector than I do, and he can turn it off when he wants to—like when it's about *himself*. Nothing is ever *his* fault; he's always pissed off at someone. Actually, it's more like he's always pissed off at everyone. Except me."

"Why not you?" Electra asks

"I told you before: he loves me. He thinks I'm perfect. He absolutely believes it.

"Ha!" Electra says. "Not that you're *not* perfect—"

I snort.

"I'm just saying—"

"Girls! Grace and Electra!" Captain Donnelly glares at us from the door of her office as we pass, and we grow quiet until the phone rings and she goes in to answer it.

"Do you know what the dictionary definition of 'belief' is?" Electra says in a low voice. "'Confidence in the truth or existence of something not immediately susceptible to vigorous proof.'"

"How do you know that kind of shit?" I ask.

"I told you. The Library. But never mind that. Here's what's interesting. Kyle thinks you're perfect, right?"

"Yeah. He does."

"Do you think he honestly *believes* that?"

"Actually," I say. "I do."

"Okay. And what do you think would happen if he put that belief to a 'vigorous test'?"

"Seriously?"

"Yeah. Seriously. What do you think would happen?"

"He wouldn't put it to a test," I say. Then, "Oh!"

"Exactly," Electra says. "Here's what I figured out. 'True believers' are the same, no matter what they believe in. Those church ladies believe in

Jesus, Kyle believes in you. They'd never in a million years put it to a test. Which is the *opposite* of a crap detector. You see what you need to see to make whatever you decide to believe work."

I have to laugh. "Kyle would be so pissed if I told him that. Him being like the church ladies, I mean."

"Well, since he's ex, he'll never know, right?"

"Moot point," I say. "I'd never tell him in the first place."

"Because?"

I shrug. "Wouldn't be worth it. He'd get all—"

Electra's eyes narrow. "He'd hurt you?"

"No. *No.* Kyle would never hurt me. Really. No way."

"Then what?"

"He'd—*argue.* That's what he does, until I get all confused and whatever he's saying starts making sense, even if I know it's totally crazy. Which is how I ended up here. "I'm not saying it was his fault. I knew what we were doing was wrong. I also knew his parents would bail him out if we got caught, and mine wouldn't. I was stupid."

"Jerk," Electra says. "He knew it, too—and he knew yours wouldn't. But he let you do it anyway. And you think he loves you?"

"I know he does," I say. "The thing is, he's a better person than you think. He really is. I just don't have the first clue what that's worth."

"Zero," Electra says. "Zilch. Nada. Nil. Nothing."

Candy Hearts

Last year, on Valentine's Day, Kyle gave me a box of custom-made candy hearts. "Amazing Grace," "Kyle + Grace," "K+G Forever," "I ♥ Grace—" sprinkled among the usual messages. We set the box between us on his bed, Kyle reading each one out loud before placing it in my mouth, then kissing me, until kissing wasn't enough and the candy spilled onto the sheets, making heart-shaped indentations on our skin as we had sex.

It was right before I realized I was pregnant, before everything got so completely out of control. I can barely remember the girl I was then. I can't bear to think about it, and, worse, I can't keep my mind from turning to Jack, who gave me a big stuffed animal and a grown-up box of candy wrapped in red ribbon every Valentine's Day.

"I love you, Grace," he'd say. "You're my girl."

The last thing I want to talk about right now—with anyone—is love. Any kind of love. But when Group meets on Valentine's day, Ms. Miller brings red fruit punch and cupcakes with white icing, dotted with candy hearts.

"What is love?" she asks.

Kaylie and Destiny giggle; Lauvette groans.

"There's no such thing," Amber says. "Just guys who pretend it because they want to have sex with you."

"Say it, sister," Kenyae says.

"I loved Damien's daddy," Jessica says, her voice trembling. "His name was Cody. I thought he loved me. That's why—" She blushes. "You know. But he was from the devil, he tempted me, and I gave in. It wasn't love I felt at all. I learned that praying to Jesus. Cody's a bad person. He pretends Damien doesn't even exist. So, what I think is, a mother's love for her child is the only real thing."

I consider my own mother, who never thinks of anyone but herself, and wonder if she might have loved me if my dad had stayed and tried to make things work. I remember Jessica's mother, strung out on drugs that day in the visiting room, and think, the sad thing is, she probably does love Jessica—she just never had the first clue about how to take care of her. I think of my own lost baby, who'd be five months old now. Would I have done any better?

A chorus of voices erupts.

"Oh, yeah," Bree says. "My mom, she just loves me to death. That's why she put me out on the street when she got a new boyfriend—with no money and no way to get any other than selling shit."

"My mama done what she could for me," Lauvette says. "I know that. She probably right now praying for my soul. But I'm the one made the choices I made."

Jessica shrinks into her chair.

Wren watches.

Ms. Miller looks sad. "Girls," she says. "There is love. There *is*. I promise you. And I believe each one of you has it in you to find it. You are here to prepare yourself for love that will sustain you through the rest of your lives, whether it's the love of a partner or a child or a friend. You're here to learn to find your best self and show it to the world. You're so young." Her voice quavers. "Your whole lives are before you. *You* control what your lives will be…"

Electra said I know things; maybe she's right. Because I know every single one of us—except Jessica—is vibrating with anger and embarrassment, thinking, *God. Why does Ms. Miller have to be such an idiot? What good could it possibly do for someone so completely clueless about everything as Ms. Miller is to believe in me?*

Big Sky

Kyle's mom sent an email to my parents:

I hope you'll consider allowing Grace to spend spring break with us at our home in Montana. Kyle is excited to show her this place he loves and teach her how to ski. We'd pay for her flight, of course, and for all of her costs while we're there. She's such a lovely girl. Both Kyle's dad and I have grown very fond of her. You can be sure we'll take good care of her.

Marlys and my dad said, "Absolutely not." It was inappropriate for a high school girl to go on vacation with her boyfriend's family—especially since that boyfriend was Kyle, who they considered spoiled and disrespectful. My mom said to them, "He's a nice boy from a good family. But if you don't approve, maybe you'd rather take Grace with you to Florida on spring break. I know she'd love spending a whole week with Briony."

At which point they decided it was okay, after all.

I dreaded going.

The way Kyle's mom acted you'd have thought we really were going on a fabulous ski vacation. She showed me the ski area website that featured a photo of their chalet, promised a "girls' afternoon" at the Solace Spa and Salon at the base of the mountain.

Kyle and I would ski the first four days, she decided. We deserved a few days of enjoyment before—

It scared me half to death just to think of the real reason I was going to Montana. Plus, I didn't want to ski. I was terrified of heights. Simply looking at the photo on the website of people going up the steep mountain on a chairlift made me anxious—and actually arriving in the little ski village surrounded by mountains sent me into a near panic. You could see too far. Where were you supposed to settle your eyes? And the mountains were so craggy, like long white knives piercing the sky.

"Is this place awesome, or what?" Kyle asked.

How could I tell him that the mountains made me feel small, Midwestern, made me see I didn't fit into Kyle's family and never would. Kyle himself seemed like a stranger here: so easy with his parents. Enthused, compliant. Like the little boy he once must have been.

Maybe I'd take a bad fall and have a miscarriage, I thought. Then I wouldn't need the abortion after all. Maybe I'd even break my leg and all I'd have to do is lie around the chalet and read, looking up now and then at the mountains framed by the windows. Kyle would hover over me, bringing me hot chocolate, attending to my every need until, nobly, I insisted that he go out and ski, at least for a while. And he'd love me even more.

The next morning, I sat sweating in the ski-rental shop, dressed in my new red jacket and the sweater and ski pants Kyle's mom had lent me, while Kyle consulted with a leathery, pony-tailed old guy. He returned carrying brightly colored short skis, which he said were the best ones for beginners, along with heavy, clunky boots that were hard to put on and virtually impossible to walk in, and we made our way toward the baby slope.

"Baby slope," I said to Kyle. "Ironic."

He gave me a blank look.

"Like why we're here? Because of a baby?"

"It's not a baby," he said. "We can't think that way. It's—"

I looked at him, decked out in his ridiculous knee-length jacket, bright blue, decorated with skulls piled on a black and white checkerboard, noticing for the first time that there was a tiny head of a creepy-looking baby with round eyes and a china doll mouth tucked among them here and there. I didn't mention this.

Or the fact that there seemed to be babies everywhere. Not actual babies, but rosy-cheeked toddlers bundled in brightly colored snowsuits, princesses and superheroes decorating their tiny helmets. They trudged toward the baby slope, their parents holding their mittened hands on the magic carpet ski lift—then precariously made their own way downhill, bent over, their skis in snowplow position, their parents skiing alongside, hands out to catch them if they started to fall. Some did fall, rolled to a stop, laughing, and their mom or dad offered a ski pole, pulled them up, and sent them off again, cheering them along the way.

"Good job, buddy!" rang out all around me.

For just an instant, I saw Kyle teaching our own little one to ski a few years from now, all bundled up, cheeks rosy in the cold, excited for this new adventure. I stopped; the real scene suddenly blurred with my tears.

"What," Kyle said. "What's wrong?

"Nothing. I don't know. I just feel like an idiot. Look. Babies can do this, and I can barely walk in these stupid boots."

"Come on," he said. "You'll be fine."

And, shocking myself, I was. A few awkward trips down the baby slope and the skis began to feel like part of my body. I felt like I was flying.

"A natural," Kyle told his parents at dinner. "Seriously. It's like she was a skier in another life. You should have seen her. You loved it, didn't you, Grace?"

I blushed, nodded. "I did."

The next three mornings, I woke up in Kyle's arms, dressed, ate the breakfast Marianna prepared, stepped into the cold, white morning, and flew, warmed by winter sun, until the last run was called in the late afternoon. Then Kyle and I lounged in the hot tub until it was time to go to dinner with his parents, who seemed to know everyone, and introduced me as Kyle's girlfriend.

"We adore her." Marianna put her arm around my shoulder, drew me close.

We walked back to the chalet, laughing and talking, the sky above us black as velvet, a riot of stars tossed upon it. I pushed back my anxiety about tomorrow's appointment, quelled the little voice inside my head. *Is it really the right thing to do? How much will it hurt?*

I would do anything for Kyle and his parents, pay any price for this kind of belonging.

Bad Karma

That morning, before skiing, Kyle and I had gone for the required counseling, where I assured the counselor I'd thought things through and was absolutely sure I'd made the right decision. I promised to read the booklet the counselor gave me, which described the procedure, defined medical terms, and outlined the possible complications. Though I didn't. What was the point? I'd made up my mind. I was going to go through with it, no matter what.

Marianna said she'd be glad to take me to the clinic for the procedure. Kyle hadn't really had a chance to ski with his dad since they'd been there and that would be a nice thing to do. "Your father's so busy," she said. "You don't get to spend enough time together."

But Kyle said, "No way. I'm going with Grace."

Marianna pressed her lips together, but she didn't argue.

There were a dozen or so people outside the clinic, holding signs. "Choose Life." "Pray to End Abortion." The predictable photograph of a mangled fetus. A man with wild eyes chanting into a bullhorn, "It's not too late! It's not too late!"

I had prepared myself for this. I kept my eyes down, kept hold of Kyle's hand. I was fine until a tree-hugger-looking girl stepped directly in front of me and raised her sign right in front of our faces: "Abortion is Bad Karma."

Kyle pushed her so hard she stumbled backwards.

"It is, though," the girl called out. "Really, really bad karma. You'll see."

I stood, shaking, until Kyle put his arm around me and gently propelled me away. "Bitch," he muttered. "I can't believe she'd say that."

I remember Marianna, waiting at the door, opening it. I remember the smell of the clinic, like any doctor's office. I remember the white walls in the waiting room dotted with cheerful framed prints of wildflowers, the uncomfortable plastic chairs. I remember standing up when my name was called and Kyle standing up, too, but the nurse saying, no, she was sorry, but he couldn't come with me. I remember following the nurse down a corridor, hearing the girl's voice in my head, "Really, really bad karma," wondering if what I was about to do really, really *was* bad karma, wondering what bad karma actually meant.

I remember not one single thing after that: not the room they took me to or the doctor or the needle used to anesthetize me. Just how weak I was, coming to. How grateful, stepping from the clinic into the frigid early evening air, to see that the group of demonstrators had dwindled, the tree-hugger girl was gone. I remember Kyle climbing into the backseat with me, guiding my head to his shoulder so I could drift off to sleep as we drove back up the mountain.

I don't remember much from the days that followed. It hurt; I remember that. And I remember how Kyle never left my side, how he sent his mom out to get grape popsicles because I loved them, how he curled himself around me to sleep.

I remember how he hummed with anger at the tree-hugger girl, he couldn't get over what she said, even when I begged him to stop talking about it—though I never admitted it was because I couldn't stop thinking about what the girl said, either.

I still think about it sometimes.

Now, in the middle of a session with Dr. Welty, I ask, "Do you believe in karma?"

Dr. Welty tilts her head, curious. "Why do you ask?"

I shrug. "That thing about how you pay for what you did in another life? What I don't get is, does it always work that way—you know, bad shit...stuff...happens because of what you did in some life you don't even remember? Or can there be payback for something you did in the life you're living now? The thing is—"

The words tumble out. "I had an abortion. I didn't tell you before. I'm sorry. But I was ashamed. I guess I still am. Anyway. There was this girl protesting at the clinic, she wasn't like the others, and she held up this sign that said, "'Abortion is Bad Karma.'"

"Oh, Grace," Dr. Welty says, one hand to her heart. "I'm so sorry you had to go through that—the abortion, the girl. It's a terrible decision to have to make, and you don't need people like that to make it worse once you've decided. When did that happen?"

"A year ago, last spring. In Montana. My parents thought I was on a ski vacation with Kyle and his parents. It was why, you know, I got so—"

Dr. Welty temples her fingers, waits.

"The thing is, I was doing okay. I'd kind of convinced myself it was the right thing, the only thing I could have done until I got home and saw Briony and it came rushing at me, what she was like when she was a baby and how much I loved her. How I might have loved my own baby the same way, I probably *would* have, but now I'd never know because I'd killed them and that girl at the abortion clinic was right, it was bad karma, the worst kind of karma. So, what else mattered?" I slide up the sleeve of my sweatshirt to show Dr. Welty the long scar on the inside of my arm. "It was stupid. As soon as I made the cut, I thought of Briony finding out I was dead, how sad she'd be, how it would mess up her life –"

"Thank heavens for Briony," Dr. Welty says. "She's like your north star, isn't she?"

I nod. "And Kyle. Well, it felt that way then. I freaked out and called him. The cut wasn't that deep. He did the tourniquet thing above it, like we learned in health class, and the bleeding pretty much stopped. I told him not to take me to the hospital, I didn't want my parents to find out, but he said, no way, we were going, and he called my mom to meet us there. I thought she'd be furious, I was prepared for that, but she wasn't. She seemed scared, she was shaking, and I felt bad for her because I could see she had no idea what to do with me."

"Your dad?" Dr. Welty asks.

"I begged my mom not to tell him because I knew he'd tell Marlys."

"And she agreed because she understood that Marlys finding out would make it harder for you, hurt you more?"

"I don't know. Maybe. Or she figured Marlys would ask people at church to pray for me—or *her*—and then everyone would know."

A silence falls between us. What is Dr. Welty thinking, I wonder, now that that the notation in my file—one suicide attempt—has blossomed from black marks on the page into another sad, pathetic story? What would *I* think if I were the person to whom the story was being told? What if my mom was telling it? All I know is that anger roared in once she knew I was safe.

Nothing changed between. Could it have been possible for the story to turn out another way?

"Did you want to keep the baby, Grace?" Dr. Welty asks, softly.

"No. I don't know. I couldn't have—" My voice cracks, and I take a deep breath before going on. "Okay, the truth is, sometimes I think I only had the abortion so my parents wouldn't know. And that was wrong. Even if the abortion was the right thing, which it probably was, it was wrong not to tell them I'd gotten pregnant."

"What do you think they would have done if you'd told them?"

"I know exactly what they'd have done," I say. "My mom would have said I should get an abortion so she wouldn't have to be embarrassed. Marlys would have convinced my dad I should go to some horrible Christian home for unwed mothers and have the baby and give it up for adoption. They'd all have argued about what to do, but mainly about whose fault it was that I got pregnant in the first place."

"Then I think you did the right thing not telling them."

I sit up straighter. "You do?"

"I do," Dr. Welty says. "From what you've told me about your parents, I don't think it would have been useful to tell them. It doesn't much matter whether they didn't care enough to help you or wouldn't have known how. I think you've come to understand that on some level. I think it may have played a part in what happened after the abortion, too.

"As for karma," she continues. "The way I understand it, it's intention that matters. Whether you made the decision about the abortion from good intent or bad."

"But I don't know which it was," I say. "I couldn't think straight. I let Kyle's parents decide."

"And what was their intent, do you think?"

"They thought having the baby would wreck Kyle's life. And mine. But his, mostly."

"Did he want to have the baby?"

"He said he did, he said he wanted us to get married and have our own family and it wouldn't be fucked up like everyone else's. But he's—well, he's always been first. *Only*. He's kind of a baby himself, you know?"

"And you'd have been the one responsible."

"Yes," I say. "And I couldn't. I just couldn't. I wasn't ready."

"Then you did the right thing," Dr. Welty says. "Which doesn't mean you won't always wonder who that child might have been. It doesn't mean what happened won't always make you sad. But think of this: If karma is true, if we really do have many lives, the spirit of your baby is still out there, not dead—just delayed—waiting for the door to her next life to appear. If you look for her along your path, you might just find her."

Caught

The house was on a wooded lot in the middle of the city. There was a locked gate at the driveway, but it was easy to climb over the low, split-rail fence surrounding the property and streak through the sea of fireflies toward the back patio.

Since the first burglary, Kyle had done research on where people are most likely to hide house keys, other than a fake rock. People put them in old prescription bottles and buried them. They attached them with magnets behind air conditioning units, tucked them into the house siding, attached to transparent fishing line. You could buy fake poop, which Kyle always hoped to find. But, so far, all the keys we'd found were hidden in fake rocks.

It was the same that night.

Kyle sighed. "Idiots." He said it every time.

I followed him into the big house, through the kitchen, its quartz countertops gleaming in moonlight, into the dining room, where Kyle slipped a silver pitcher and a silver platter into the pillowcase he was carrying. Then the huge living room, with white couches and Persian carpets on the wood floor, dark shadows of trees framed in the windows. There were paintings on the walls, some small enough to carry, but we never stole art. Kyle said that would be wrong.

We went up the stairs, the treads creaking beneath us, but it didn't matter, I reminded myself. The people who lived here were in Paris; Kyle had heard them telling his parents about the trip when they came for dinner the weekend before.

In the master bedroom, there was a canopy bed with burgundy draperies pulled back to reveal a matching comforter, a tumble of decorative pillows. Kyle took a photo of the couple when they were teenagers from the collection on the high dresser, I took the tortoise shell hairbrush from the dressing table and an especially ridiculous Limoges box: a plaid sneaker with a gold clasp in the sole.

What is it about rich people and little boxes? I wondered.

We'd undoubtedly find Mont Blanc pens in the man's study, when we got to it, along with the fat Cuban cigars in glass tubes rich men loved. Kyle always took one of those to smoke on the way back to his house. Just one. He wasn't greedy.

We ranged around the bedroom, opening and closing drawers and doors, but the couple must have kept anything of real value in a safe—maybe behind one of the paintings in the living room. Kyle picked up a Swiss Army knife, a German stein in the shape of an alligator. He slipped the TV remote into his pillowcase, just for fun.

I found a pistol in the drawer of the bedside table and held it up for Kyle to see, rolling my eyes. That was the other thing about rich people: Even the ones who said they believed in gun control often kept a gun near where they slept. I guess because they had so much to lose.

I turned to put it back into the drawer but froze at the sound of a creak on the stairs.

Kyle heard it, too. "Shit," he whispered. "Motherfuck. Put that thing *away.*"

But it was too late.

I saw him first and screamed—dropping the pistol.

The policeman held a gun in both hands, just like in cop shows, pointing right at me.

"It's not mine," I said. "The gun. *Please.* I'm telling the truth. It's not. I found it—"

"Quiet," the cop said. "Both of you. Hands on your heads. You kids are goddamn lucky I didn't shoot you."

And as I raised my hands, the door across the hallway opened and I saw the terrified face of a girl. She was wearing cat pajamas, her long hair tousled from sleep, her cell phone in one hand. She was maybe twelve, not that much older than Briony.

"Oh, no," I said. "Oh, my God!" I started forward, as if to comfort her.

The cop took a long step, grabbed my hands and cuffed them behind my back. Then Kyle's. He read us our rights, again, just like on TV.

Meanwhile, a second cop appeared and knelt before the girl in the doorway. "You did a good job, honey," he said, in a low, kind voice. "It's okay now, you're safe. Where are your parents?"

At which point, she burst into tears, and so did I.

"*Fuck*," Kyle said, near tears himself. "I'm really sorry. They were supposed to be on vacation. We never would have—"

Shut up, I wanted to say to him. But I couldn't stop crying to say it.

"Seriously," he said. "We didn't think anyone would be here."

"Well, doesn't that just make everything all right," the first cop said. "You little shit. You think it's okay to break into someone's house and steal their stuff, as long as you don't scare them?"

"No," Kyle said. "That's not what I meant—"

The cop turned his back and joined his partner in reassuring the girl and, finally, she calmed down enough to call her mom. Her parents were at the hospital, she said, waiting for her mom to pick up. They didn't go on vacation because her grandma got really sick. They'd let her stay by herself just this once, she said.

"Fuck," Kyle kept saying. "Fuck, fuck, fuck."

I wondered if he even knew he was saying it.

I'd stopped crying but my nose was running, my face wet, and all I could do was shrug up one shoulder and try to wipe it on my hoodie. My wrists hurt. The plastic cuffs were too tight. And when I heard the first faint sound of a siren, my bladder gave way. The hot urine traveled down my legs into my sneakers; I gagged at the ~~cloying~~ smell of it. I thought of holding the gun in my hand, what might have happened if I hadn't dropped it, and I began to shake.

The girl, still standing in the doorway of her bedroom, watched me—and I knew that as long as I lived, I would remember that first sight of her, the fear on her face that I had put there.

A girl who might have been my sister.

TWELVE

Day 100

I've looked forward to marking out the '100' on my calendar, assuming that this milestone, finally reaching just double digits of days left, would make me feel good. And the act of marking the day out actually does. Then it's lights out and I lie there, sleepless, the ninety-nine days still left lined up across my mind like an impenetrable fence. And WTF am I going to do when I *do* get out? It's not like either of my parents is dying to claim me. The thought of seeing Kyle again makes me feel sick with dread. Going back to school makes me feel even worse.

I wake up on Day 99 in a foul mood, with a pounding headache. Jessica's cheerful "Good morning" makes me feel murderous. The cold rainy day feels like a personal insult, and I slump into a chair in the cafeteria, look at the food on my tray, and it's all I can do not to pick up a handful of slimy eggs and throw them at the wall.

Then Officer Snap appears as we're lining up to walk to the Promise Academy and bellows, "Lowery, come with me. You're wanted in administration."

Shit. I wrack my brain trying to figure out what I've done wrong.

There's a moment of silence, then murmuring as I cross the cafeteria. Nobody's been called to administration the whole time I've been here. It must be something really bad. No hint from Officer Snap, who grabs my upper arm like usual, leads me through the door and down the corridor without a word. Outside, I pull up the hood of my jacket, put my head down against the rain, and do my best to keep pace with Officer Snap, hurrying to deliver me to my fate.

The lights in the administration building seem eerily bright in the gloom of the morning, the corridor still shines with last night's polish. It's one of the original hospital buildings, heavy oak doors and carved molding where the walls meet the high ceilings. One day, when we were supposed to be working on a research project in the library, Electra googled the mental hospital. Apparently, when it opened they brought in six-hundred patients from Indianapolis by train.

"You'll love this," she said to me. "The guards had shotguns loaded with rock salt, in case they got out of control. Jesus. They might as well have been prisoners, like us. And they gave people electric shock here, which was horrible then. I've seen it in movies. It practically electrocuted you. Seriously. It burned up your goddamn brain." She was as angry as if it had happened yesterday to someone she knew.

Officer Snap stops at one of the doors and gives me such a hateful look that I flinch. Then puts her professional face back on and knocks.

"Here's your girl, ma'am," she says to the woman who opens the door.

The warden, Ms. Farrell—I recognize her from a photograph at the entrance of the Promise Academy—thanks Officer Snap, then gestures me into a conference room. There's a long table at the front with two people seated there, name plates that say, "John Harvey, Commissioner" and "Renee Yates, Commissioner." The warden points me to the single chair in front of them and takes her place at the table.

John Harvey looks like a guy who's been in charge of things all his life: big, well-dressed, a gold fountain pen poised above the papers before him. Renee Yates is plain, bony, with lank mouse-colored hair flat against her head. Probably one of those girls tormented by the popular kids in high school, and now here she is with the power to make a whole lot of girls' lives miserable.

The warden looks anxious.

Mr. Harvey clears his throat. "Miss Lowery," he begins. "We have brought you here due to a change in your status at Madison Valley that came to us from the governor's office."

"*Governor's* office?" I say. "But—"

"You are here to learn of this change," Mr. Harvey interrupts. "Not to discuss the who, what, or why of it. Do you understand?"

"Yes, sir. I do."

"All right then. The governor has decided to change your release date."

I hear a strangled sound come from my own throat and, suddenly, I'm back in the bedroom the night of the last robbery. I feel the weight of the pistol in my hand.

The gun should make a difference, the prosecutor had said at my hearing. Your Honor, Grace Lowery had a gun in her hand when the police officer came upon her in the bedroom of the Andersons' home. There was a child in the house who might have been harmed by it.

The judge, by some miracle, had not given me the maximum sentence allowed. But I should have known the gun—the stupid, stupid gun—was going to catch up with me, after all. The Andersons had made it clear they weren't happy with the sentence. They're powerful people, so they've gone to the governor—

"…reduced," Mr. Harvey says. "Your release date has been changed to May 19, twenty-eight days from today."

I'm so stunned by the news that I only half-hear him outline the procedure of my release, how the governor's decision can be rescinded at any moment, *any moment*, if I fall out of compliance with the rules of the facility.

"It is extremely rare for the governor to interfere with the work of the Prison Board," Ms. Yates adds. "*Extremely* rare. You would do well to pay heed to what Mr. Harvey is telling you about falling out of compliance. Believe me. You won't be this lucky a second time."

Not the Andersons, after all. They're powerful, but not as powerful as Kyle's family. It was Marianna who went to the governor, then. I'm absolutely sure of it.

"You don't belong in a place like this," she said when she visited in the fall.

No doubt she said it again and again in the letters I tore into little pieces before reading them. Of course, it was Marianna. She'd have felt perfectly comfortable going to the governor to get what she wanted—slipping him an envelope with a generous campaign donation in it and a note. *For your enduring commitment to the good people of Indiana.*

I start to shake and, suddenly, I'm cold, so cold. My teeth chatter and I clench my jaw, but they keep chattering anyway; I feel like I might be sick.

"Not so special, after all?" Office Snap says, when I'm dismissed to her care. "Got a dose of the real medicine in there, did you?"

I'm still shaking. I must look like I've just been given a death sentence, which I figure is a good thing because it means she doesn't know what happened. But she will. So will the girls in Cottage Five—and the minute they find out they'll get on my case about being a rich girl again and do everything they can to make me fuck up. And why shouldn't they? It's not fair. Most of them did nothing but harm themselves with drugs to end up here, while I committed real crimes.

Then there's Jessica, whose heart will be broken, who will mourn my going before I'm gone and make me feel guiltier than I already do.

Oh. And Electra.

"I saw Commandant Snap take you away," she whispers when I get to class. "What happened? Are you okay?"

"Stupid bureaucratic stuff," I whisper back. "I'm fine."

The relief on Electra's face assaults me. I shouldn't lie to Electra, of all people. She'd be glad for me; she could be trusted to keep it to herself. But I just can't bring myself to tell her right now.

I have to get my head around what happened first. Twenty-eight days. I'm furious at Marianna for calling in favors for me. Kyle *himself* hates that kind of thing, though it makes me even more furious that he'd probably think it was fine in this case—

But I'm also reeling with gratitude and relief—and joy so wild and unwieldy that it's frightening.

How will I keep it a secret?

PAWS

"Grace!" Jessica says, bursting into the dayroom. "I just had my review and guess what. That dog thing? PAWS? Where you get to take care of a dog and, you know, teach it stuff?"

I nod. I can see the kennels, in a far corner of the compound, from the window of the math classroom, the dogs running and playing in their own fenced-in yard.

"Well, guess what? They chose me! Can you believe it? *Me!* The lady who's, like, in charge—Ms. Boseman, she works at the animal shelter—anyway, she took me to the kennels and, oh my gosh, the dogs are so, so cute. And jumping all over you because they get so excited—which we have to teach them not to do. We get to go every day! After school."

She's like a puppy herself, writhing with happiness.

"That's so cool, Jessica," I say. "I'm really glad for you."

Then glare so hard at Maria for mimicking Jessica's excitement, and at Bree and Adrienne, hands to their mouths to quiet their laughter, that the three of them shut up and look down at their books, pretending to study.

"You should see Patsy," Jessica says, oblivious. "She's the one who's going to be mine. She's so soft and she licked my hand, just like a kiss. You'd just love her. I can't wait to tell Damien about her. Ms. Boseman said she'd take a picture of me and Patsy to send him.

"I'm for sure going to get us a dog when I get out. And I'll know how to take care of it. PAWS is going to be so fun. I can't wait till Monday, when we start. You should ask if you can do it, too."

"I'm allergic to dogs," I lie. "So, I can't."

"Oh," Jessica says. "I'm really sorry."

The truth is, I'd love to do the PAWs program if I was still going to be here. I love dogs. I've wanted one ever since I was a little girl. Every Christmas, every birthday it was the only thing I asked for. But no. Then my dad let Briony get Ted, which proved once and for all that he loved her more than me.

It wasn't Briony's fault. She said Ted could be my dog, too, but dogs know who their person is and Briony was Ted's person. From the time he was a puppy, he'd curl up as close to her as he could and gaze at her adoringly— which he never did with me. I was there so rarely, he probably didn't even know I was part of the family.

Just thinking about how much I wanted a dog when I was little makes me want to put my head on the table and sleep. Not to mention lying to Jessica. But the program lasts twelve weeks and I'd have to tell Jessica about my new release date to explain why I can't be in it.

I tell myself that Jessica getting into the PAWS program is like the cosmos saying *Yes!* not only to the news of my release, but to keeping it a secret. She'll fall in love with Patsy—she already has, and when I leave it won't hurt as bad.

Meanwhile, I try to be kinder to her, less impatient. To listen—really listen—to her talk about Damien. I celebrate her passionate devotion toward Patsy, which truly is endearing. Of course, she's convinced that Jesus brought Patsy into her life, but as the days pass she talks less about Jesus, even less about how much she misses Damien. Instead, she talks about Patsy's shiny coat, what a sweet temperament she has, how her tail wags wildly, like a helicopter, the second she spots Jessica coming through the kennels gate. She comes back to Cottage Five every day bursting with pride about all she's teaching Patsy to do. She can already sit and stay and shake hands! And she's learning to walk on the leash, even though she doesn't like it.

"I mean it," she says. "Patsy is way smarter than the other dogs. She's going to get the special gold star on her Canine Good Citizen Certificate, I just know. Some people, though. Like this girl, Randi? She's teaching her dog to fall down and roll over when she says Bang, and everybody else thinks it's so funny. But I don't think that's right. It's like violence, you know? And isn't that what we're supposed to be learning is bad in here?"

"It is," I say. "I bet Ms. Boseman thinks the same thing."

Jessica beams. "She *does*. She told me Patsy's going to be the kind of dog the forever families want and that's all on account of me."

I feel punched in the gut. And when that happens, who will mend Jessica's broken heart?

A Dream

I dream I'm eleven again, and my tiny new breasts grow and grow until they are bigger than my whole body. I don't know what to do with them, they won't fit in my clothes anymore, they drag behind me when I walk. My mom says, "For god's sake, Grace, they are so ugly, they're embarrassing, can't you make them stop?" and I try to explain that they're the only things keeping me safe from Jack, but my mom says, "It's your own fault Jack doesn't want to see you anymore. It's always something with you. You're always whining about something and who wants to listen to that?"

"But I don't *want* to see Jack anymore," I say in the dream. "I'm afraid of him, he hurt me, he's been hurting me for a long time and—"

"Nobody's hurting you but yourself," my mom says. "You're impossible, you really are. And I mean it. Do something with those ridiculous breasts right now."

But when I try, they turn into snakes, coiling around my neck, hissing, "Don't tell, I will kill you if you tell."

I wake up, gasping, scared to death until I remember I'm locked in a cell and what I'm really scared about is who might know about my early release date and what they might do to make sure I serve every single day of time—or more.

At breakfast, the smell of eggs, the slop of them on my plate and the half-cooked bacon make me nauseous. I'm hot, then cold, then hot again. I stand up to take my tray to the conveyor belt and feel dizzy. I stand still, my eyes closed, until my equilibrium returns. Afterward, I'm grateful to walk into the raw wet air, even though it makes me shiver.

I feel sluggish walking the Shape Up Zone track.

"What's up?" Electra asks. "You look like shit."

"I'm getting out early," I say. "Fourteen days."

"For real?" Electra asks. "*That's* why you look like shit? Are you crazy or what?"

"Kyle's mom did it. She had to have been the one to make it happen. That's why I didn't tell you before now. Because it's so unfair."

"Fuck fair," Electra says. "Like life's ever fair. But I hear you. Does that woman not know how things *work* in a place like this?"

"People do what she wants. Period. That's all she thinks about."

Electra shakes her head. "Fucking rich people. Who else knows?"

"I'm not sure. I don't think anyone in the cottage knows. Look. I'm really sorry I didn't tell you—"

"Don't worry about that. Worry about getting your ass out of this place in one piece. I'll get out of this dump eventually, then watch out world."

"You'll come find me, right?" I ask.

"Yep," Electra says. "I will."

What Dr. Welty Knows

Does Officer Snap know? She glowers at me when she comes to pick me up for my appointment with Dr. Welty later that day, clamps her meaty hand over the ever-present bruise on my arm and manhandles me out of Cottage Five and onto the sidewalk. "You watch yourself, Lowery," she says in a low, mean voice, giving my arm one last squeeze, before knocking on Dr. Welty's door. "You're not done here yet."

When the door closes behind me, when I'm safe in Dr. Welty's office, I sit down and begin to shake—*again*. My teeth chatter so hard they ring inside my head. I can't keep doing this; I have to learn to control my body. But I can't stop until Dr. Welty gets up from her desk and puts her hands on my shoulders.

They feel so good, gentle and firm at the same time, hands I know will never, ever hurt me, hands I can curl up beneath, drawing my knees to my chest, wrapping my arms around them until I'm like a big baby in a womb.

"There's something I need to talk with you about, Grace," Dr. Welty says, when I've calmed—and my first thought is, *shit*. My release date. But when I ask if there's a problem, she looks confused. "I'm pretty sure Kyle's mom talked the judge into it," I say. "She's like that. And the hearing was weird. Like they knew. So I thought maybe—"

"Everything's fine with your release date," Dr. Welty says. "You just need to be very, very careful until the day comes."

"I know. There's no way I'm doing anything to get myself in trouble."

She nods.

I wait.

Then, something passes between us, not words, and I know Dr. Welty has figured out what happened with Jack. Not that it's Jack, she couldn't know that. Just that it happened. I'm practically bursting with relief. I trust Dr. Welty with my life, I can tell her anything. *Everything.*

But as if she knows what I'm about to let it all spill out, she raises a hand. "I called you in to talk about where you'll go when you're released," she says. "I'm worried about the tensions in your family, how they might affect you if you go back to live with your mom. You'll be eighteen soon. Would you consider going to a group home until then?"

I get it. I remember Kyle telling me how, if you're not eighteen, you should never, ever tell a therapist anything you don't want your parents to know. They have to tell Child Services if it's about violence or abuse and Child Services has to tell your parents. It's the law.

"It's a good place," Dr. Welty says, as if she needs to convince me. "You'd be treated with respect, they'd help you get yourself together, get ready for what comes next. And you'd be allowed occasional visits with your family. Grace——?"

"Yes," I say. "*Yes.*"

Then it occurs to me. "What if Marlys won't let me see Briony?"

"I can't promise what will happen with Briony," Dr. Welty says. "But from what you've told me about her——" She smiles. "My guess is she'll wear them down eventually. Don't you think?"

I laugh for the first time in what feels like forever. "Yeah. There's a pretty good chance of that."

"The group home then?"

"Yes."

"And on your eighteenth birthday, I want you to make an appointment with my friend, Dr. Truitt," Dr. Welty says. "She's agreed to see you on a pro bono basis as long as you need it. You'll tell her about——" She raises her hands, as if to stop herself. "That's five months from when you leave here. Do you think you can manage until then?"

"I *will* manage," I say.

And for the first time in a long while, I know exactly what to do: meet each morning, calm and unflappable, put one foot in front of the other, walk through one day and the next and next until the gate opens and I walk through it back into my life.

THIRTEEN

Jessica Gets a Letter

Jessica jumps up when her name is called and practically runs to get the letter Officer Hadley is holding up for her. "Thank you, ma'am," she says. "*Thank you.*"

"I bet there's pictures of Damien," she says to Grace. "My mom promised to take him to see the Easter Bunny last Saturday, she's been working a lot, that's why they haven't been for a while, but I really wanted Damien to see the Easter Bunny, even though I miss him so much—"

She opens it, but there are no pictures, just what looks like some kind of bill with writing on the other side of it. "Grandma," Jessica says and, as she reads, all the color from her face drains away. "No," she whispers. "No. Oh, no."

Then hands me the letter and begins to howl.

I can barely read it, the writing is so small and cramped—and its long, run-on sentences like Jessica talks, and even worse spelling.

Honey its real bad news your moms in trubil again I dint no I thot she was better she was working I thot thats why she was leaving Damien with me so much but she wasnt working she got with those people you know the ones. The sheriff come to get her and take her back. She knew better, I guess she couldn't help it, but honey heres the thing I jist cant keep Damien with me. I love him to peces you know that but I barly have enuf to get by and my arthritis I cant hardly get arond anymore and the lady from the sheriff office said theres good people who can keep him better than I can until you come home and get a job and set your life right I know that wont be too long and hell be waiting for you the lady promise. I prayed on it hard and God said yes it was the right thing to do so Damien gits what he needs, good food and clos and going to the doctor if he gits sick like he does sometimes them ear akes you know poor little guy he gets so many of them. I cried myself sick when they took him but he was a good boy and he dint cry the lady had toys for him you should of seen his face he was so exsited and I seen it was the best thing. Dont you be sad honey, you pray on this like I did and youll see everthing will be okay you be good too so you can come home for him your not going to be like your mom honey I know that and I hope you do to on acont of Damien needs you and I miss you something teribil. Gramma

Every eye in the dayroom is riveted by Jessica, who keeps howling, rocking back and forth, her hands raking her hair. Even Wren looks up from her book. I sit there, the letter still in my hand, and all I can think is *No Touching Allowed.*

Officer Hadley kneels beside her.

"No," Jessica shrieks, flinging out an arm, knocking her backwards.

There's a collective gasp, a long murmuring.

"Leave me alone," Jessica wails. "*Leave me alone.*"

But she's not in trouble for it. Officer Hadley rights herself, nods at me—and I give her the letter. She's a good person, Officer Hadley. After she reads it, she leans in toward Jessica and says in a voice so low only I can hear, "I'm so sorry Jessica, I know how much you love that little boy," at which point Jessica slumps down, hands to her face, sobbing. She lets Officer Hadley take her to the office and pretty soon Officer Snap arrives to take her somewhere, maybe the infirmary, where I hope they'll sedate her at least for a little while.

All the other girls are looking at me, waiting for me to tell them what the letter said, but fuck them. They're all awful to Jessica. Why should I tell them anything? I put my elbows on the table, cradle my head with one hand as if to resume my homework, and only when tears start running down my forearm do I realize that I'm crying.

Something There Is That Doesn't Love a Wall

Of course, word gets around about what was in the letter.

"Somebody take my baby girl," Kenyae says, "I be killing them."

"Uh-huh," Lauvette says. "I be right there with you, sister."

I didn't even know Kenyae had a baby. She never talks about it.

Later, Ms. Miller brings up Jessica's letter at Group. "You all need to be kind to her when she comes back," Ms. Miller says. "You know how much she loves her son. But sometimes we have to do what's best for our children, even when it hurts."

Amber, who never says anything, turns bright red and sits straight up in her chair, glaring. "Bullshit," she says. "Like foster care is better for kids. Believe me, I know it's not. They get paid to take kids in. That's all they fucking care about."

"Amber!" Ms. Miller says. "Language! And not every foster family is—"

"Yeah, well, every foster family I ever went to was. And worse. Use your imagination about what that means," Amber says. "I'll give you a hint: "Night. Daddy." She nearly spits out the word "Daddy."

"Been there," Bree says.

"Me, too," Adrienne chimes in. "I'd kill anybody who tried to send me back."

I almost feel sorry for Ms. Miller who for a moment looks like she can't breathe. Is she really that out of it? Or in a terminal state of denial, like

Marianna who continues to think Kyle is a genius, the perfect son, despite the evidence piling up to contradict this. I'm convinced that when Marianna looks at him, she sees the bright, sweet, curious little boy he once was, not the spoiled, stubborn, sullen teenager he's become. Maybe, when I was little, Marlys saw the difficult, ill-behaved child she needed me to be? To my mom and Aunt Marjorie, Jack was a kindly would-be uncle who enjoyed my company.

This should piss me off, I try to be pissed off, but all I can feel is sadness so heavy that my very bones seem to be crushed by it.

I remember how my sophomore English teacher always harped on point of view. It was everything, she said. It was why reading fiction mattered. It let you live inside the head of someone who wasn't you, to see the world through their eyes. If you couldn't do that—if you didn't even try to do that—you'd never really understand anything. I thought it was an interesting idea at the time. Now, suddenly, I see the deeper meaning: there is no one, single world. Nothing that can be verified in any way that matters. Knowing anyone, really knowing them, is as unlikely as waking up one morning to find that hate and greed and the terrible hunger for power have magically vanished, leaving everyone, *everyone* at peace with one another.

"Yes," Dr. Welty says when I share this observation the next day. "The question is, does that mean you should stop trying to make peace or you should try even harder?"

"Or get what you need for your own world," I say. "Then build a big concrete wall around it."

Dr. Welty smiles. "'Something there is that doesn't love a wall—'"

That same English teacher had made us read the poem that line came from—and I'm transported to the classroom, kids arguing for and against walls. The teacher—what was her name?—interrupting to quote, "'Before I built a wall I'd ask to know/What I was walling in or walling out/And to whom I was like to give offence.' What do you think about that?"

213

"Build a gate with a lock," someone said. "You can let people in if you want to."

"And who cares if someone gets offended? That's their problem." Monica was the one who said that.

"Offense might also mean hurt," the teacher said. "Whom the wall might hurt."

Monica shrugged.

"Do you know the poem?" Dr. Welty asks now. "'Mending Wall.'"

I nod.

"It's a favorite of mine. Such a simple situation, repairing a wall after a hard winter, but everything of life is in it. A good poem is like that, you know? So small. But everything is there, everything is true—even things that seem to contradict themselves. And so often made from pain," she adds. "Trying to understand pain."

I sigh. "I've been trying to build a wall to keep Jessica out ever since I've been here," I say. "She keeps knocking it down. I feel so bad for her, about losing Damien—about her whole *life*. But I don't want to be friends with her. She's so, I don't know, it's like she's got her skin on inside out. She sets herself up to get made fun of. She lets people hurt her when she shouldn't care because they're—awful. Some of them are really, really awful. But I just can't be responsible—"

"Is that what Jessica expects? For you to be responsible for her?"

The question had never occurred to me. "I don't think so," I say. "She's never acted like she does. But I *feel* responsible for her."

"You're not responsible for Jessica, Grace. You can't control what happens to her or how it feels. If you take responsibility out of the mix—?"

"She just wants me to be nice to her," I say, miserably.

"Which you are," Dr. Welty says. "From what you've told me, I think you are."

"But I'm not, always. Sometimes—she just drives me crazy."

"I'm guessing Jessica forgives you for that," Dr. Welty says. "If she even notices it."

"That's the thing: she probably doesn't. She's dead set on the idea that I'm perfect. Oh, *God."* I say. "Just like Kyle. Totally screwed up people think I'm perfect."

"Or," Dr. Welty says, "people whose pain lets them see through you to your true heart."

But You Said Jesus Loves Us, No Matter What

Jessica is like a zombie when she gets back from three days in the infirmary. I sit with her in the dayroom, trying to cheer her up, reassuring her that she'll get Damien back once she gets out and gets her life on track.

"And you're *going* to do that," I say. "Remember all the plans you've made."

But Jessica won't talk about Damien, won't talk about anything at all. She won't go to the kennels to take care of Patsy.

"Why should I?" she says. "I'm just going to lose her, too. I might as well lose everything at once."

She won't even go to fellowship. If she went, she'd pray to be forgiven for not taking good care of her own sweet little boy, which she doesn't believe she should be forgiven for. So, what's the point?

"But you said Jesus loves us, no matter what," I say to her.

She doesn't answer.

"You could go and pray for Damien," I say. "Pray that he got sent to a good family, to people who'll love him."

"I know," Jessica says—and begins to sob, hiccupping, stumbling over her words. "I know I should pray for that. But I can't. He's so little. If they love him, he'll love them back. He'll forget me."

"He won't," I say, my own voice cracking. "You're his mom, he won't forget you."

"He will." Jessica stops crying, but her voice is wobbly. "Which is for the best. Him forgetting me. I know that, too. I mean, maybe his foster parents will adopt him, and he'll have a real family, maybe even brothers and sisters. Not just me and my grandma and my mom, when she's not on drugs. All of us with awful jobs, if we even have jobs, and never enough to give him what he needs.

"But I'm just not ready to let him go, I just can't—not yet. I just can't believe I'm never, ever going to see him again."

To comfort her, to say she's wrong, of course she'll see Damien again, she'll get him back when she gets out of this place and all her dreams for a life together will come true seems like a lie. How could that happen, really? So, I don't say anything at all. Just envelop her in a hug, which Officer Hadley sees—and allows.

Wednesday Morning

The morning bell screams me awake. The feeble overhead lightbulb goes on, cheap fuckers—and no window, so who knows what crappy weather we'll be trudging through to breakfast.

I drag myself out of bed, shivering, pull on my clothes, slip into my scuffed-up sneakers and bend to put the Velcro tabs in place. Velcro. Like we're kindergartners who can't tie our shoes. I think about the mouse droppings I saw yesterday in the dining room. This whole place disgusts me, grimy at the edges, just short of being truly gross.

Just days, I tell myself. Days.

But right this second it seems as if I'll be here forever.

I make my bed, grab my toothbrush and toothpaste, wait for the loud click of the doors along the corridor unlocking. When I hear it, I open my door, step out, stand to the side looking straight forward. That's the rule.

The count-off starts—

One. Two. Three. Four.

Ha. Like one of us might have escaped during the night.

I close my eyes, concentrate on holding my thighs together as tightly as I can until I can get to the bathroom. It's not until the silence after "thirteen" that I sense Jessica's absence. I risk turning my head to the right, where she should be standing. She's not there.

The silence deepens as Officer Hadley walks her room, opens the door, and enters.

"Oh!" she says, backing out. "Oh, dear God. No."

Into the silence, she claps her hands and orders—

"Back to your rooms. Now. Close your doors behind you."

Nobody moves.

"Right. Now."

The sound of doors closing all along the corridor, the loud click of lockdown.

Then the squawk of radios, pounding feet, the rattling wheels of a stretcher—

And Jessica, covered with the green army blanket from her bed, framed in the tiny, barred window on my door. Then gone.

Paperclip

I'm crying, I've been crying all day. In my room, in lockdown; on trips to the bathroom, going one by one so we can't talk to each other; through breakfast and lunch delivered to my room (cold scrambled eggs, soggy toast, and a watery cup of orange juice; a peanut butter sandwich, limp celery sticks, a carton of warm milk.) I cry, following the unsettlingly subdued Officer Snap to Dr. Welty's office; cry harder at the sight of Dr. Welty's face. I'm overwhelmed by gratitude for having been called there, to sink into the chair in Dr. Welty's quiet office with its shelves filled with books, photographs of loved ones smiling, its window framing the blue, blue sky.

Dr. Welty looks as if she might have been crying herself. Her voice cracks when she says, "I'm so sorry, Grace. Ah. This *place*—" She shakes her head. "Tell me—"

"How?" I interrupt. "How did she do it."

"A paper clip."

Jesus. A paper clip. You'd have to gouge yourself with a paper clip.

And no question about how Jessica knew the right way to use it: girls whispered about suicide all the time. Just a few group sessions ago, Amber had made fun of a girl in another cottage. "Fucking loser," she said. "Everyone knows you cut up and down, not sideways."

Jessica never mentioned the up and down scar on my forearm, but had she noticed it? Was that part of how she knew?

It makes me feel sick to think of Jessica sitting on her bed, unbending the paper clip Just the first part, so the rest of it, the metal oval, would be like a little handle; or maybe all the way, creating a tiny spear. Did she sharpen it against the cement wall first? Sharpened or not, did she plunge it into her vein right off, or work herself up to it: first a long scratch, then going deeper and deeper until the blood gushed? How long was she conscious, lying there believing that she'd done the one thing Jesus would not forgive her for, believing she was going to burn in hell because of it, never to be reunited with Damien, who would someday go to heaven?

Christians, I think. Why would they make people believe something so horrible? I could kill that fellowship woman who I absolutely know will pray when she hears about Jessica's death, but not asking Jesus to forgive her—oh, no—asking him to take the leftover girls into his hands and keep them from committing such a sin themselves.

And what stupid staff person left a paper clip where Jessica could find it? When did she find it? Had she found it a long time ago, maybe even before

I came, and hidden it somewhere in her room, just in case? Had it appeared the day she found out about Damien—an omen, a gift? If I believed in Jessica's Jesus, I'd pray for the first. It would make me feel less to blame, though I'd be lying to myself to leave it at that because, what if Jessica had found out that I was leaving soon, leaving her alone here with nothing in the world to hope for now that Damien was gone? What if she used the paper clip because of that?

But of course, like so many things that matter desperately, it is impossible to know.

"It wasn't your fault, Grace," Dr. Welty says, bringing me back. "There's no reason to think it had anything to do with the fact that you'll be leaving soon. You didn't tell Jessica, did you?"

"No. I didn't tell her."

"And there's no reason to think that any of the other girls in the cottage knew, right?"

Meaning, I knew, if they had found out, they'd have relished outing me, relished watching Jessica learn that I'd kept this secret from her.

"No. Not that I know of," I say.

"What Jessica did was about her little boy," Dr. Welty says. "We don't need to talk about this now, but I want you to keep the sound of my voice in your head saying this: Jessica's suicide is not your fault."

But it *is*. If I'd been Jessica's real friend, if I'd said, "I'll help you get Damien back when we get out." But I don't have the strength to argue.

Dr. Welty fixes me a cup of chamomile tea, the same kind of tea Kyle's mom fixed for us when Kyle was in a good mood and we sat with her in the studio for a while. The scent of it brings back Marianna's paintings with their beautiful indistinguishable words. I hold the warm mug in my hands, raise it to my nose and breathe it in, my eyes closed.

"Here is my concern," Dr. Welty says. "I know you're grieving. I know that, despite what I say, you feel responsible. And I also know how it can go in a cottage when something like this happens. You're all going to feel out of balance, you're all going to deal with what happened to Jessica differently, and those differences are going to create tensions that can pretty quickly explode.

"You can't afford to lose control of yourself, Grace. Your release date is less than two weeks away. You absolutely can't risk jeopardizing it. You know that, right? And you also know you can't afford the thought that acting out, forcing the board to change its mind about the date, would result in the punishment you think you deserve."

I glance up sharply. How did she know what I was thinking?

A ghost of a smile plays on her face. "I'm asking you to promise me that you will do everything in your power to avoid any kind of conversation about what happened to Jessica with the girls in Cottage Five, unless it is in direct response to something Ms. Miller asks you in group. And, even then, be very careful."

"Okay," I say. "I'll try."

"Good," Dr. Welty says. "Drink your tea then. Let's both of us relax a little while before I send you back there."

FOURTEEN

I Heard about That Girl

"I heard about that girl from your cottage," Electra says. "I heard she did it with a paperclip—and if that's true, Fuck. She really wanted to die."

"It's true," I say. "She did. It was Jessica."

"What?" Electra stops short on the track, just steps into our walk.

I glance toward the proctor, nudge her forward. "It was Jessica," I repeat.

"Oh, man. *Shit.* That's awful. But listen to me, Grace. You were *so* not as big a shit to her as you think. You were nicer to her than anyone else was. But here's the most important thing. If Jessica hadn't managed to kill herself this time, if someone had stopped her—you, anyone—she'd have done it eventually. Listen. Hanging out in shelters, being on the street, I know about this shit. You need to believe me."

I want to believe this; on some level I do believe it. But I keep going back—I can't stop—to goddamn Ms. Miller, who called a special group session not long after Jessica's body was discovered, then blubbered her way through it, grieving Jessica's belief that death was the only option, pleading with us never, ever to consider such a thing ourselves.

"Everyone, everyone has moments when they believe things are hopeless," she said. "But there is always hope. You have to be strong enough to keep looking for it. To find it.

"I'm just so sorry that Jessica didn't—" She took a Kleenex, dabbed her eyes. "I think—let's all say something about Jessica, shall we? To remember her, to celebrate her life. I'll start." She attempted a smile. "She loved that little boy. Nobody ever loved a little one more than she loved him. And she was a friendly soul."

"That girl be talking the angels in heaven to death now," Lauvette muttered. "That's all I got to say."

Ms. Miller ignored her. "Grace," she said. "You were her friend—"

The others turned toward me, daring me to speak.

I didn't. But Jessica's hopeful expression the day I arrived in Cottage Five was burned into my brain: a new person, someone who might not be unkind to her. And I hadn't been unkind, not like the others. I hadn't made fun of Jessica, or purposely done anything to hurt her. I put up with Jessica because I didn't know how not to, I helped her with her homework to pass the time. But I hadn't really been Jessica's friend.

"Well, I'll pray for her," Ms. Miller had said, into the stubborn silence. "I hope you girls will, too. God help her."

At which point, Wren started to laugh. Not that she was sitting in the group circle. She never actually attended Group, just sat, reading, nearby. Or listening, I suddenly realized. All those times she sat outside the circle she was listening.

Officer Hadley left her desk, knelt next to Wren, and whispered something into her ear. But Wren just kept laughing, peals of laughter that made her roll over and clutch her stomach—and pretty soon the girls in group were laughing, too.

Except me. I was speechless, rooted in astonishment.

Ms. Miller flapped her hands in alarm.

Officer Hadley helped Wren to her feet—and Wren's laughter stopped short, as if Officer Hadley had pressed an off-button. Her face took on its familiar blank expression. The girls stopped laughing, too, watched the two of them disappear into the corridor, then slumped back into their usual group positions as Ms. Miller took the opportunity to talk about how close laughing and crying were to each other, how Wren was probably really crying about Jessica, maybe they all were. It was such a tragedy what had happened to her.

Jessica hasn't been mentioned in Cottage Five since.

Rumor was that Wren wasn't sent to solitary, but to the infirmary, where she was sedated, and would be kept there until she returned to her quiet, unresponsive self. But nobody knew for sure.

"Grace?" Electra says, bringing me back to the track. "Grace?"

I take deep, gulping breaths to keep myself from crying. "I hate this fucking place so much. I can't believe you—"

"Whoa, whoa, whoa! I never said it was the Hilton Hotel."

I laugh, a little hysterically.

"Shh." Electra glances toward the proctor. "I said it was better than foster homes, better than the street. Which is a fucking low bar. But there's something else, Grace. There are some people who can't live in this world. They just can't. And I don't know. Maybe if that's the case, they're better off, well—*not*. I know that sounds terrible. But I think it might be true."

"Maybe," I say. "Which is the most depressing thing of all."

"Yeah," Electra says. "Except nobody can ever hurt Jessica again. She's not sad anymore. She's not anything at all."

223

The Last Time

Not at his house, not in the special bedroom with its books and stuffed animals, not in the closet where Cathy stayed until Jack dragged her out. Not on the bed with its yellow comforter and pretty pillows.

It is winter, sleeting against the car window. There is the sound of the windshield wipers, the radio on low: weather advisory, heavy snow coming, stay off the roads unless absolutely necessary. But Jack keeps driving in the opposite direction of his house. I don't recognize the neighborhood. Run-down houses, stores with signs written in Spanish. A twinge of pleasure mixes with my anxiety because I'm learning Spanish at school. I can read some of the words. Normally, I'd tell Jack. He'd be proud of me; he might take me to the bookstore to get a book to practice. He likes it when I learn things. But for some reason I don't tell him, and pretty soon we're out of the city, on the interstate, and there's nothing but frozen fields on either side of the road, an occasional farmhouse, although I can hardly see them because the snow has begun to fall. It's like looking at the world through one of those see-through curtains. Why do people have those? I've always wondered. Either leave the window bare and let people see in or cover it up.

Jack slows down, pulls the car into the empty parking lot of a rest stop, and turns off the engine. He gets out, goes around and opens my door. Holds out his hand. What can I do but take it?

"We need to have a talk," he says. But he doesn't talk. Not right away.

He keeps holding my hand. We go up the sidewalk, into the low building where there's a rack of flyers: places to visit in Indiana. A map of the state takes up one whole wall. There's a red star near the middle of it and the words: "You Are Here." Signs point to the women's bathroom, the men's. There's also a sign that says Family Bathroom, and that's where Jack takes me, locking the door behind us.

"You will be quiet, Grace" he says. "You will not say a word. Because I want you to remember."

I feel my body folding into itself.

Jack puts his hands on my shoulders. "Stand up straight."

But I can't help it, my legs don't work, they fold me down to the floor. He kneels beside me and I lie rigid as a doll while he takes off my coat, my shoes, my tights, my school uniform, my panties, the itchy bra I don't really need yet but my mom said I should have because I'm not a little girl anymore. Slowly, slowly, looking at me the whole time. He doesn't take his own clothes off, he never does. I close my eyes against the sound of the zipper, press my lips closed, but there it is with its soft skin, opening them, and I do the thing he always wants me to do, the thing I hate most, even more than when he puts it in my girl place and pushes and pushes and it hurts so much I want to scream.

When he's finished the air changes above me, he's no longer in it.

Zip.

"Put on your clothes," he says.

I am eleven years old. I'm embarrassed by the new breasts budding on my chest. I'm not used to them yet. I know Jack doesn't like them; he's never said but I can tell by the way he puts his hands flat against them, as if to make them invisible.

"Open your eyes," he says.

I hadn't realized they were still closed.

"Stand up."

In a voice I've never heard before, he says, "I will say this to you one time: If you tell anyone I brought you here, if you tell anyone anything—*anything*—I will bring you back to this place, do what I just did, and then I will kill you."

I hear a quiet sound come out of me, breathe it back in.

"Do you understand?"

I nod.

"Say it," he says. "Say you understand."

I whisper, "I understand."

And that is the end of it.

Spokane Means Children of the Sun

"We talk so much about unhappiness in therapy," Dr. Welty says. "It's what gets you here, after all. You never see a long line of happy people at a therapist's door. But everyone has happy moments, *everyone*, and it's important to give them weight, too. What made you happy, and why. When and where you were happy. Who's in your happy memories. Who's *not*. So, let's take a break from sadness, shall we? Let's talk about something good that happened in your life. It doesn't have to be perfect; nothing is. Just something—or part of something—that makes you happy to remember."

And I remember Camp Sleeping Bear.

I didn't want to go, but there was no more Jack Camp after Jack got tired of me, and my parents had to find someplace else for me to go when school let out. It was the summer after fifth grade. Still friends with Zoe then, I worried she would forget all about me and only want to be friends with Monica when I got back. And I'd never been away from home by myself, I wouldn't know a single person there. I felt carsick most of the long drive to Michigan, I tried to sleep, but couldn't, and my mom had to stop the car so I could throw up when I saw the sign for the camp.

Then we got there, and pretty soon I felt better. It was because of Lolly.

She was tall, with blond hair in a long braid. She'd come to Camp Sleeping Bear every single summer when she was a kid, it was her favorite place in the whole world. Now she was in college and she was the counselor for my cabin. The cabin was named Spokane and Lolly said it was the best cabin of all and we were lucky to be in it because Spokane means "Children of the Sun."

I thought the lucky part was Lolly.

The first night, sitting around a campfire, she told a story about a mother bear and her cubs. They were hungry, so they tried to swim to Michigan, which was rich with plenty, but the baby bears were too weak and they drowned. The mother was so sad and tired all she could do was lie down and look out at the water. But then, right before her eyes, the Great Spirit Manitou made two islands come up in the places where the baby bears died and after that a high dune so she could watch over them forever.

Some girls were afraid they might see a bear, but Lolly said the black bears that lived in Michigan were shy and rarely came anywhere near the camp, plus they were vegetarians and didn't eat people even if they were really, really hungry.

"But what if we do see one?" a girl asked.

Lolly said, "If you're in the woods I'll be with you because you're not supposed to be there without me. If we see a bear, I'll start talking in a normal voice so the bear knows we're humans and then we'll all slowly, slowly back away. So, you don't have to worry."

But I wasn't worried about bears. I was worried about Jack. What if my mom or Aunt Marjorie told him where I was? He was a science teacher. He knew about the woods. He could sneak through them and find me to make sure I wouldn't tell someone in this new place.

I will kill you if you tell. I couldn't stop hearing him say that.

I was afraid to go to sleep. I heard noises through the open window: the whoosh-whoosh of wind in the trees, water splashing lightly on the shore, rowboats knocking against the wooden dock, the call of an owl. It smelled different here, like trees and water. The sky was so black, I'd never seen sky that black before and the stars in it so bright. Jack could come right in the open window and cover my mouth and take me and nobody would know until morning when they woke up and I was gone.

Then I heard footsteps coming close. I couldn't help it. I breathed out a quiet cry and curled up quick like a roly-poly bug—*armadillidida*, little armadillo, Jack had taught me in one of his science lessons—and closed my eyes as tight as they would go and waited for his hand to come over my face.

But it wasn't his hand. It was Lolly's hand. And not on my face, on my shoulder. She said, "Wake up, Grace. It's me, Lolly, you're having a bad dream. Don't be afraid, you're right here with me in Spokane Cabin, safe. There's nothing to be afraid of in this place. I promise."

And I had a feeling inside like a huge ball of string coming untangled.

I can't remember the last time I thought about Lolly, but now she appears, fully alive, in my mind, and the ache of missing her is as powerful as it was when camp was over and I had to go home. Something in me has missed Lolly ever since then, will always miss her, though I didn't realize it until this moment.

I remember Lolly leaping off the dock into the freezing cold water, screaming and waving at us to come after her, and we did, one by one, screaming, too, and swam toward her like baby ducks. I remember Lolly in the cabin the night before field games chanting, "We can do it," and pretty soon we were all chanting—and the next day we did it, we won—and Lolly was so proud of us. And how Lolly let us take turns braiding her long hair, how she whispered to me that I'd done the best job. I remember standing behind Lolly, the sun-warm strands of her hair in my hands, the mixed-up smell of the lake and woods and shampoo and something I couldn't name but thought of as Lolly herself.

Breathing in that smell when Lolly hugged me.

"I went to summer camp when I was eleven," I tell Dr. Welty. "In Michigan. Sleeping Bear Dunes. And my counselor, there, Lolly—"

Dr. Welty smiles, maybe at the name.

I thought it was a funny name, too, when I first heard it.

"She was so pretty and nice," I go on. "And she wasn't afraid of anything. So, I wasn't either, when I was with her. When I told her that near the end of camp, she said it didn't surprise her. She'd seen the moment I got out of the car that I was afraid, but she also saw that I was a brave person inside. She said it was her special power to see brave people and ZAP their bravery right out of them into the world, which was why she was really glad when my name was called for Spokane Cabin. I totally believed her."

"There are people like that," Dr. Welty says. "With that power. I believe in them."

"You do?"

"I do. And I agree with Lolly. I think there's enough bravery inside you to last a lifetime."

"No," I start, "How—"

"I don't know how," Dr. Welty says. "I'm just telling you what I see, what you don't—can't—see yet. You were brave to be Jessica's friend when the other girls didn't like her, when they made fun of her."

"But I didn't *want* to be her friend, I just couldn't make myself not be."

"Which means you were following your conscience. You know, Grace, courage is tricky. It can feel like weakness, like giving in, because you listen to the voice telling you to do something you don't want to do. But that thing can be the right thing. More often than not, it's also the hard thing. You did the hard thing with Jessica. You cared about her."

"Yeah, but in spite of myself."

"That counts just the same."

"How can it? It's like taking credit for...a mistake."

"It counts," Dr. Welty says, firmly. "You're not responsible for what you think or what you feel. You're not responsible for not wanting to be Jessica's friend. You're only responsible for what you did—and, in Jessica's case, you did what you could."

"Right. And look what happened." My eyes well up with tears.

"Grace," Dr. Welty says. "You made Jessica's time here better than it would have been. That's what you need to remember. You know—" She smiles. "I'll bet she thought of you the way you thought of Lolly. Did you go back to the camp after that summer?"

"No. The next summer was that awful church camp I told you about."

"Oh, dear," Dr. Welty says. "What an awful contrast for you. But I'm glad you have that wonderful memory to balance it out. Because here's what I think about happiness, Grace. It's not a state of being. It's an accumulation of happy moments. Like one of those add-a-pearl necklaces. The more moments you have, the more beautiful the necklace becomes, the more weight it carries. So, it's important to remember those moments, to add them up, especially when things are at their worst. Sleeping Bear Camp was one of those for you. There are others."

There's a black leather notebook on Dr. Welty's desk and she picks it up and hands it to me. "Write the moments that have made you happy, anything that's ever made you happy, no matter how small—maybe even something that made you happy here." She raises her hands, palms out. "I know," she says. "That's a stretch."

"In any case, the book is yours. I'll instruct the staff that nobody is allowed to read it. But you know I can't absolutely ensure that it won't happen, given where we are, so keep that in mind."

I open it: graph paper, my favorite kind. And the smell of paper. I rifle the beautiful blank pages and memories begin to float up.

And in the evenings, when I used to sit with Jessica, I write.

Necklace of Happiness

Zoe's mom gives us diaries on Valentine's Day when we're nine. Pink, with hearts on them, and "My Diary" on the front. But the best part is, there's a lock and a tiny key to open it. "You can write about all your happy times together," she says.

And, oh! I remember the time Zoe's dad took us to fly kites in the park. They were rainbow kites, he bought one for each of us and sent them flying. It was windy with a blue sky and sunshine. It was March, but so warm we took our jackets off and left them in the grass. I remember the tug of the kite in my hands, thinking what if a really big wind came and I got lifted right off the ground—and I wasn't scared, I even wanted it to happen. I'd grab Zoe's hand and we'd fly off for a big adventure. Then her dad would find us, and he'd be so glad we weren't lost that he'd buy us ice cream and say, "Of course you're not in trouble, the wind did it, it wasn't your fault."

I am standing in front of the mirror in my bedroom, striking different poses, saying, "My boyfriend. My boyfriend, Kyle. My boyfriend said—. My boyfriend has a Jeep. Kyle, my boyfriend, and I get coffee every day after school, he says he needs a fix. "My boyfriend, my boyfriend, my boyfriend." It's like a song, I can't stop smiling.

Kyle: skiing.

Kyle: skipping school the first time, dashing across the parking lot to the Jeep, laughing.

Kyle's voice saying, "Amazing Grace."

That beautiful dress laid out on his bed.

My mom is getting ready for a special dinner. She's getting an award, a big one, she told me, for selling more houses than anybody else at her work. She loves selling houses, it makes her happy, but the award is even better than selling the biggest house ever, except she is nervous because she will have to go on stage and say a few words. I know because I heard her tell Aunt Marjorie. I don't know what the words are, but her mouth is moving just a little, and I think maybe she's practicing them in her head—like I practice my spelling words. She looks so pretty in her glittery black dress, perfume floats all around her like a cloud. When she walks across the room, her shiny black high heels leave dots in the carpet, like tiny animal tracks—and she stops when she sees me watching and says, "How do I look?" and I say, "Really pretty, Mom," and she gives me a little kiss on my forehead before she goes down the stairs.

Briony's hand. When she was in kindergarten, all the kids made clay plaques of their hands to give their parents for Christmas, but Briony didn't want to give her hand to her parents, she wanted to give it to me—and Marlys had to let her do it because she wrote "Grase" right in the middle of the palm. It's red clay with a bumpy white glaze on it that looks like botched-up icing, but I love it more than anything.

School: the letters of the alphabet marching across the wall above the whiteboard, every word in the whole world right there—I just had to learn how to put them together to make the ones I wanted. How numbers fell into place and became answers. How I always knew what to do to make the teacher like me.

Kyle's mom's paintings, the feeling of almost, almost being able to read the word-like scribbles but not actually being able to read them, which makes me believe, that not everything in the world needs to be understood. Sometimes beauty—what beauty does inside you—is enough.

Electra bolting, running, throwing herself into the pile of leaves.

Dr. Welty's office: the warm cup of chamomile tea I hold in both hands.

Jessica's sentence diagram: "I love Damien."

Zoe and Monica had a huge fight, I don't even remember about what, just that they were screaming at each other and then Monica left, slamming the bedroom door behind her. Zoe said, "I hate her. She's so bossy, she thinks she knows everything, I'm glad she's gone." She got out her Barbies, which we both knew we were getting too old to play with, but we didn't care, and for the whole rest of the afternoon, it was just the two of us, like we used to be.

Belle: how her face lit up when I got off the school bus, the smile in her voice when she said, "Honey! I've been waiting for you all afternoon." How, when Belle was in the house, I knew I was safe.

My dad, before Marlys. I remember him coming home from work each day, the door opening and there he was and he'd smile and open his arms when he saw me and I'd jump into them. I remember the feeling of him being there, in the house, and how I was always happy when he was there. But is that really the way it was, or is it just some trick of longing?

Nana, though. Everything with Nana is happy. And real.

Then this: When I keep being sad because she's gone Jack takes me to Walmart and says I can get whatever I want—and what I want is the yellow ball at the very top of this whole big cage of balls. "How about blue?" he asks. "Or red?" Because there are blue and red balls close to the mouth of the cage, also green and orange. But I only want yellow because yellow is my favorite color and Nana's, too, and I start to cry because the cage is way taller than Jack and I know he won't be able to reach it. "None of that!" he says. "Yellow it is! Watch this." Then runs our grocery cart right into the cage and knocks it down and my yellow ball bounces down and lands right at my feet. "There you go," he says. I'm so shocked I can't even say thank you, like I know I'm supposed to do. I just pick up the ball and hug it to my chest, like it's Nana herself, right there, taking care of me.

I put down my pencil, shaken by a rush of happy memories of Jack.

Floating in the swimming pool, his hands beneath me, holding me, the sun warm on my face. Jack mimicking a bird song while we're hiking in the woods, he sounds just like it—then telling me its name. And naming the stars we can see through the triangle of tent flap, the tent he set up in his backyard piled with pillows and blankets, the two of us spending the whole night in it and I wasn't one bit scared, even though I was still little enough to be wearing footie pajamas, because Jack was right there with me.

Stop, I tell myself. *Stop.* But the memories keep coming—and for the first time, I see that, while Jack did terrible, unspeakable things to my body, the worst thing he did was to make me happy, make me love him, all the time waiting, waiting for the moment when he could be sure that my love for him was more powerful than the bad things he'd known he was going to do to me all along.

I *was* happy with Jack in the beginning. I did love him. And just now, remembering, I feel like the happy little girl I had been with him then.

That happiness wasn't real, I tell myself.

But it *was.* Then.

What am I supposed to do with that happiness now?

I think of the matching Tibetan prayer beads Kyle bought for us: onyx with three tiny silver skulls interspersed among them. "Skull stations," he said they were called. When your fingers touched the skulls, praying, you were meant to remember the brevity of life and the limitations of human understanding. Not that either of us used the beads to pray. We wound them around our wrists to make bracelets.

Kyle's mom smiled when she saw them. "Cool," she said. "Going steady in the new millennium."

Which, of course, annoyed Kyle.

At the time, I was still in a state of astonishment about how suddenly my life had changed, how Kyle had known instantly that he loved me. Sometimes when I wasn't with him, when I began to doubt that it could really be true, I'd unwind the beads from my wrist and let them dangle from the palm of my hand and, eyes closed, finger them one by one, thinking kyle kyle kyle kyle kyle, like a mantra. The skull stations didn't scare me. When I felt the cool silver beneath my fingers, I thought *now*.

Now was everything, Kyle said. Nothing mattered but now.

But every single moment in my life, happy and sad, some with undercurrents of danger, had brought me to now: locked up in this bare room with nothing but my own thoughts. To forget even one of them—if that was even possible—would be to forget myself.

So, I'll give each happy memory of Jack a rough bead in Dr. Welty's necklace of happiness to remind me how much they cost. To remind myself of who I am, the strong, courageous person I will become in time—because and in spite of them.

Spring Comes Anyway

Spring comes anyway. That's what I think, walking in line to school just a few days before my release. It's a chilly May morning, snowdrops and crocuses defiantly thrusting up in the brown grass, trees just beginning to green up. "Look, Grace!" Briony had said when she was really little. "Look! The trees are putting on their green dresses." I have to keep my hands behind my back to keep from taking Briony's postcard from my pocket to look at it, but I feel its presence there.

Harry Potter World: Diagon Alley, lined with quaint store fronts—Quality Quidditch Supplies, Weasley's Wizard Wheezes, Madame Malkin's Robes for All Occasions—its gleaming cobblestone street inviting you to enter. Briony's writing on it is tiny and gets even smaller the closer it gets to the bottom.

Dear Grace, The Hogwarts Castle ride was awesome, but it made my mom throw up. She was MAD. There was a Butter Beer stand, and I had some. It was good. (But not real beer.) I saved up my money, plus Mom and Dad gave me some so I got a lot of stuff: a Hogwarts hoodie, a Gryffindor tee-shirt, also socks, also a patch for my backpack, chocolate frogs (which I ate all of), the Marauders Map, a Quidditch Golden Snitch necklace. I got a stuffed Dobbie. It is so, so cute. I got Hermione's wand and Sirius Black's wand. The Sirius Black one is for you. (I said I couldn't decide and faked crying because I didn't have enough money for both and they gave me more. Ha. Ha.) Love, Briony.

Of course, Briony chose Hermione's wand for herself. She's like Hermione: spunky and smart. Loyal. Stubborn in all the right ways. She doesn't understand why my favorite character was Sirius Black and I'll never tell her it's because of something Sirius said to Harry—about how Harry wasn't a bad person, he was actually a really good person who had really bad things happen to him. How when I read those words I wondered—and still do—if I might be such a person myself. How the words live inside me.

And the part about how we all have light and dark and what matters is which we act on.

Now some dark magic takes me back to that last afternoon with Jack: the click of the bathroom door locking, his cold hands undressing me, the cold tile floor beneath my back. His panting, his sour breath.

"I will kill you if you tell anyone."

Then, suddenly—*Whoa!* I know without a sliver of doubt that Jack won't kill me. He wouldn't dare.

"Lowery. Get a move on."

Officer Snap, who else? Her hand on the riot stick in her belt.

Like a wand, I think—and smile.

I move on, thinking of the magic wand that awaits me, a gift from my sister, who loves me no matter what, who first brought forth the light inside me.

Wren Speaks

It's been over a week since Jessica killed herself, since Wren was taken away, laughing, and Cottage Five still feels like the inside of a can of soda that somebody shook up hard. Who's going to open it?

Idiotic Ms. Miller, who outed me at the end of her last group session yesterday?

"I know we all wish Grace well in her new life," she said. "I know I do—and I know she will manage beautifully."

A sudden alertness, the muttering told me that the girls in Cottage Five hadn't known I was leaving until that moment.

"Thank you," I said, as if I weren't afraid.

They won't do anything, I tell myself. They're not going to trigger an outburst to get me in trouble because it would mean shutting Cottage Five down with demerits for everyone—or worse.

It's just days now, I remind myself. Just days.

For once I'm glad for the nightly meds that dull my mind and make me drowsy. When they kick in it's as if someone untied a knot at the top of my head, loosening each muscle from my forehead down to my toes. My breathing evens out. I feel the air letting out of all the girls, too, which means they won't have the energy to hurt me. At least, not tonight.

The next afternoon Wren comes back. Officer Snap delivers her to Cottage Five, handcuffed, and Wren stands perfectly still while Officer Snap unlocks them. Released, her hands fall to her sides like a puppet's. She's so tiny, I think. She looks like a little girl next to Officer Snap. Her flyaway white hair, her arms and legs like twigs.

Conversations cease, board games stop mid-play, girls look up from their homework. The only sound is the television blaring. Officer Hadley touches Wren's arm and Wren moves toward the corner of the couch where she always sits, where nobody dared sit the whole time she was gone. She takes the battered copy of *Harry Potter and Goblet of Fire* Officer Hadley offers to her but doesn't open it. Instead, she sits looking at us, her light blue eyes settling first on one girl, then another, as if to remember where she is, who we are. When she gets to me, the ghost of intention ripples across her face.

"You sit by me," she says.

Officer Hadley nods, giving me permission, and I go sit beside her.

Wren touches my hand briefly, her fingertips ice-cold, then surveys the room.

"If you hurt Grace, I will kill you," she says. "You know I can."

There's a collective gasp, all heads turn toward Officer Hadley to see what she will do.

She does nothing.

Wouldn't It Be a Shame to Have Missed Being Wholly You?

Electra is in solitary again, she won't be out until I'm gone—and though I don't know what Electra did to get in trouble, I'd bet she did it on purpose so we wouldn't have to say goodbye. I get it. I've been dreading that moment myself. And we've made a plan, so it's not as if we'll never see each other again. When we're both eighteen, off probation and free to make our own choices, Electra will message me on Facebook. We'll share an apartment, get a dog and name her Patsy and, one way or another, make it through college together.

Still, I wish I could have seen her one last time.

I'd like the girls in Cottage Five to know I wish them well. I hope Wren knows I'll never, ever forget that fierce moment of friendship in the dayroom.

It's strange to be sitting on a wood bench in the guardhouse, alone, waiting for the state cop to arrive to take me to the group home. I feel ridiculous in the clothes the intake officer returned to me in a plastic bag. Black Sabbath, really? And my once-tight Juicy Couture Jeans are loose. I lost weight here and didn't even realize it. The lacy black underwear Kyle bought for me is itchy, my feet are freezing in my flip-flops. My black hoodie isn't enough protection against the chilly morning. Because, of course we'd have an impromptu cold-front at the end of May in Indiana.

From where I sit, I can see girls in the yard on the way to school, the trees bursting into green along the high fence, already beginning to obscure the river behind them. There's the faint sound of dogs barking in the kennels in the far corner of the property. Which one is Patsy, I wonder. She was part hound, Jessica told me—

"She sounds like this," Jessica said one evening in the dayroom, and attempted a bark/howl that set us both laughing.

A bead of happiness. I smile, and at the same time I'm engulfed by sorrow.

"Is it like this for everyone?" I asked Dr. Welty the last time we met. "The way nothing is ever just plain happy?"

"It is," Dr. Welty said. "Though some people learn how to press back the sadness, see only the positive. Some go through their whole lives that way."

"And that's bad?"

"It can be dangerous. Refusing to see what makes you sad—or angry or whatever—doesn't mean it isn't there. One day something is bound to happen that brings it up, all of it, and you're in no way prepared. It's also, well, less than human to live that way. You're going to be this particular person, *Grace*, just once. Wouldn't it be a shame to have missed being wholly *you?"* She gave a little shrug. "If for no other reason than being curious about who you might turn out to be?"

I *am* curious.

Who will I be when I'm free to confront Kyle, which I know I'll have to do eventually? Even though things turned out so badly, loving me, showing me I'm someone worth loving, he gave me the first piece of my true self, and I want him to know that. But do I still love him and, if I do, is there any point in it? I guess that will depend on whether he's changed, or capable of changing enough that we might be friends until we know ourselves well enough to love each other in a better way.

Who will I be, telling my new therapist the story of Jack? Who will I be when it's told and I gather up the courage for the next thing, which is to do whatever I have to do to make sure Jack never hurts another little girl?

All I know is that I am going to do it.

Just as I know, one way or another, Briony will always be a part of my life.

And that my parents and Marlys may never love me, but they will respect me one day.

I will respect myself.

Here, now, life is coming at me so fast it's making my heart race, making me feel short of breath—a little afraid. I remember Kyle's trick, the one I used the very first day in this place: Focus on one small detail, breathe in, breathe out, looking at it. Then look at something else.

One single cement block in the wall. White, shiny. Little pock marks.

Fire extinguisher. Red.

Gray linoleum. Black and white speckles.

Brown table against one wall.

Clear plastic bowl with keys in it.

Net bag of Easter eggs. Pastels. Blue and pink and yellow and green.

Box of plastic gloves.

Square keypad next to the gray steel door leading into the facility.

Sign next to it. Bold black letters: "You Must Be In-Control Trained to Enter This Door."

Steel mesh on the window framing the State Police car turning off the highway now, heading toward the guard house to collect me and take me back into the world, where I will learn to love myself and make my own way.

THANKS

Over the course of several summers, Dr. Darolyn (Lyn) Jones and I taught series of writing workshops for teenage girls incarcerated in the Indiana Juvenile Correctional Facility as part of the Indiana Writers Center's Memoir Project. Their intelligence, wit, wisdom, and stoic hopelessness about their futures moved me beyond measure. Knowing that most of them would have been channeled into therapy if they'd been born into middle- or upper-class families made me wonder how and why a privileged girl might end up in such a place—and how she would survive. About Grace grew from that question and, while none of these girls or their personal stories appear in the book, it resonates with all they taught me. I am forever grateful to them.

Thanks to fellow writers and readers whose careful reading of early drafts was invaluable, including Betsy Childers, Joan Corwin, Barbara Davis, Margaret Love Denman, Bryan Furuness, Janine Harrison, Cara Howard, Sarah Layden, Melissa Fraterrigo, Melody Mansfield, Michael Poore, SJ Rozan, James Still—and, especially, Candace Denning, Alison Jester, and Susan Neville.

Thanks to Querencia Press for giving *About Grace* a home and to Emily Perkovich for her thoughtful editing.

And to Steve, always—for everything.